# *choose*
# HAPPINESS!

EILENE!

HAPPY & HEALTHY
HOLIDAYS 2020!

# *choose*
# HAPPINESS!

## THE PERSPECTIVIST'S HANDBOOK

*a guide to Practical Perspectivism
and happy daily living*

## JEFFREY ZAHN, MD

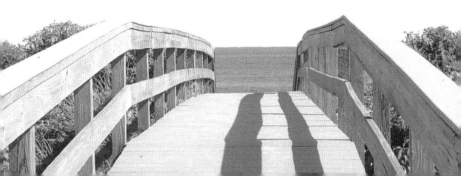

Practical Perspectivism is a philosophic ideal, a simple way of life conceived by Dr. Zahn, elaborated as a means to find and spread happiness in our shared world.

Contact: thepracticalperspectivist@gmail.com

Library of Congress Cataloging-in-Publication Data

ISBN-13: 978-1490498874

10 9 8 7 6 5 4 3 2 1

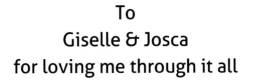

To
Giselle & Josca
for loving me through it all

I guess it doesn't matter anyway...

—*Morning Dew*, Bonnie Dobson

When I went to school, they asked me what I wanted to be when I grew up. I wrote down 'happy'. They told me I didn't understand the assignment, and I told them they didn't understand life.

—John Lennon
or Goldie Hawn
or Linus van Pelt

# CONTENTS

# CONTENTS

# PART I

# PRACTICAL PERSPECTIVISM:

# HOW TO APPLY IT
# TO EVERY DAY LIFE

# CHAPTER 1

# INTRODUCTION

It is commonly accepted there are two sides to every story (at least). I'd like to suggest this notion is just the beginning.

Our worlds, both the personal one and the larger world around us, sometimes seem to run smoothly and sometimes less so, or seemingly not all. Sometimes it's hard to discern why, what has changed, and what we can do about it, presuming of course we'd generally prefer the smoother version over the rockier road.

Practical Perspectivism (PP) is designed to demystify the complexity of events occurring in our lives, to simplify our understanding of our personal place in the "scheme of things," and, most of all, to serve as a compass to guide us back to, or even better, keep us on that smooth road, despite whatever dark alley we may find ourselves meandering near or down. More than just an abstract philosophy in and of itself, PP is a guiding principle to live by daily, an attitude to develop that engenders a simple approach to life enabling individuals to fully enjoy easy times as well as to navigate successfully through difficult waters without sinking. Rather than going off to meditate a couple of times a day to achieve a particular calm state (a practice that can be highly effective in its own right), PP shows us how to live life as, essentially, a constant meditation—a continuous mindfulness of possibilities and of our true desires.

Practical Perspectivism elucidates the limitless ways any situation can be perceived, and empowers us to freely choose which viewpoint we wish to adopt as our own. Through this mode of thought, we recognize how the shifting landscapes and events of our lives routinely lead us to adopt different approaches, sometimes subtly, sometimes more apparent. And once we recognize this is an approach we *already* utilize commonly at a subconscious level, we can both raise this awareness to a conscious level when circumstances demand greater mental focus, and can otherwise continue to allow this process to guide us unincriminatingly at its natural subconscious level.

Drawing on centuries of eastern and western philosophy, psychology, and modern neuroscience, Practical Perspectivism communicates ideals and allows us to tune these ideals to the daily art of living. In turn, Practical Perspectivism is a tool to be used to find, and stay on, your own personal path of happiness (or whatever path you choose to travel).

**Who is this book for?**
Anyone who has ever felt like there must be "more" to life will be able to achieve that sense, a deeper appreciation of all the moments of their life, by applying these ideals.

4

Anyone who has been vexed by the ancient big questions of life, like "Who are we?" "Where did we come from?" "Where are we going?" and "What's our purpose?" will undoubtedly find comfort applying Practical Perspectivism to either the answers they come up with, or to leaving such questions unanswered.

Anyone who simply wishes to be able to achieve some measure of emotional stability in their life—especially if they find their emotional responses often get in the way of their enjoyment of the day-to-day or the general currents of life—will find a measure of grounding from, and value in, living Perspectively.

And finally, perhaps most importantly, anyone who believes they could be happier, or should be happier, than they are with whatever—how much or how little—they've got will be able to easily apply the tenets of Practical Perspectivism to the attainment of this simple goal.

It is also my hope that this treatise is viewed as an addition, at some level, to the bulk of human philosophic thought. I am cautiously confident that cogitators of all stripes will take this text as something other than simply a self-help book—which in its most applicable aspects it certainly is. At least in some degree, this book seeks to address issues that arise from classic eastern and western philosophies and religions, in addition to psychology and neuroscience, while perhaps shedding new light in its own right. Furthermore, in current social writings, there exists a growing body of literature on modern Humanism—that is, secular, individual evidence-based thought rather than established faith-based doctrine as a basis for morality in general. Practical Perspectivism touches on these issues as well.

While *this* discourse on Practical Perspectivism is not intended as a rigorous therapeutic program for individuals with profoundly dysfunctional psychoses or neuroses, I remain confident the vast majority of humanity, each of us with our own array of idiosyncrasies and maladaptive behaviors (which may at times meet criteria for the realm of functional neuroses) can still benefit enormously from taking to heart, and practicing, the ideas herein.

The presentation before you is organized into two parts. The first is an explanation of Practical Perspectivism and how to apply it in your daily life. This carries on through Chapter 5. The remaining chapters, from *Perspectivism and Happiness* forward, cover a more conceptual, philosophically oriented discussion of why happiness is a worthy goal and details some of the work recently advanced in the fields of psychology and neuroscience, in particular the areas of happiness and neuroplasticity respectively. Also reviewed in the second part are some of the relevant philosophical constructs that contrast with the applied philosophy of Practical Perspectivism.

Those reading this simply for tips on how to be happier need not necessarily wade through the more esoteric final chapters. A thorough reading of the first part, especially Chapter 3: *The Ten Precepts of Practical Perspectivism*, will give these individuals enough tools to begin to increase their happiness. Those seeking a more evidence-based background discourse on Practical Perspectivism, or interested in critiquing the approach or validity of Practical Perspectivism, may well find their questions covered in the latter segment. Admittedly and naturally, the material in this second section is perhaps less pertinent to daily life. My own personal feeling is that the two parts hang together well and support each other, but I also hope each stands well enough on its own.

I look forward to your commentaries.

# CHAPTER 2

# HOW THIS BOOK CAME TO BE

## THE HAPPIEST MAN

I tell you I'm the happiest man I have known—
most happier still when I've just writ a poem—
perhaps happier yet when days gone past
and I like when I read what I've just written last.

And I'll tell you I'm not the strongest by far—
I've not a grand mansion or a sporty sports car;
There are smarter people by the countryful sure,
but there's no one more happy or happier more.

There's features with which Adonis gained fame,
and players who can't be outplayed at their game.
Presidents, kings, prime ministers, dukes—
they've all got so much and so too much to lose.

But there's one thing that's no one's to give or to take,
and it's not something one can easily fake,
for it's far deep inside where you can't fool yourself—
it's of happiness I speak, that jolly old elf.

So the choice is your own, there's no scapegoat:
on the sea of joy do you sink or float?
All I know is I'm the happiest man
I've ever met in all the land.

I wrote that poem as a lark back in September 2005. I tend to vacillate between really happy and ridiculously happy, but that's just me, and on that September day I must have been in the more ridiculous state. I've been this way for a very long time.

Even then, before I wrote this poem, before the notion of formally writing about Practical Perspectivism came to be, I had been living a life of choice, and living life in a state of happiness. But it wasn't always so.

When I was very young, they tell me, I was indeed a happy baby and child. I could play for great lengths of time by myself. As I was growing up, my parents always told me they didn't really care what I did with my life as long as I was happy. I didn't need to please them, and they did not have to like my life choices. All they wanted was that I should be happy.

In retrospect, my parents' persistence in conveying this notion that I, not they, was responsible for my own happiness served me very well. Surely, they were in part seeking a measure of independence for themselves. Nonetheless, their mantra clearly provided me a base on which to build the structure of Practical Perspectivism.

In my awkward teenage years I suffered doubts and emotional agony like most adolescents. These were dark times. And then, from the depths of one particularly bleak moment in my sixteenth year, I came to understand that those outside events, the vagaries of school and the emotional state of my peers, were matters beyond my control. They were not things that should excessively impact my sense of command over, and responsibility for, my own personal emotional state. Happiness was mine at last!

## THE ROAD NOT TAKEN

Two roads diverged in a yellow wood,
And sorry I could not travel both
And be one traveler, long I stood
And looked down one as far as I could
To where it bent in the undergrowth;

Then took the other, as just as fair,
And having perhaps the better claim,
Because it was grassy and wanted wear;
Though as for that the passing there
Had worn them really about the same,

And both that morning equally lay
In leaves no step had trodden black.
Oh, I kept the first for another day!
Yet knowing how way leads on to way,
I doubted if I should ever come back.

I shall be telling this with a sigh
Somewhere ages and ages hence:
Two roads diverged in a wood and I—
I took the one less traveled by,
And that has made all the difference.[1]

—Robert Frost

No doubt, the preceding poem, by perhaps the greatest American poet, Robert Frost, had a tremendous effect on me as a budding writer back then. I still recite it whenever presented with the slightest opportunity. It covers, simply, three of the most important concepts covered in this treatise: perspective, choice, and responsibility, all on a simple walk in the woods.

There was a brief period of my life as I finished high school and went to college when I tried to convince anyone who would listen that this way of living, personal responsibility and choosing happiness, was something doable and worth doing. But as an 18 year old who hadn't actually been living that way for very long, I was understandably not an authoritative source.

I often heard back then that my happiness was fake, it couldn't last. People said I hadn't suffered real tragedy yet, I had hardly lived yet, and that I couldn't know about true sadness or happiness. But I did know something about adversity and misfortune.

My best friend died in a car crash when I was 18, and my mother died of lymphoma when I was 20. In fact, my mother's life, and death, only served to reinforce my convictions. My mother, like her mother before her, was a worrier. Classic Jewish guilt, I guess, or something like that. She suffered from ulcerative colitis, a disease process known to be exacerbated by stress and anxiety, which was diagnosed when she was 40 years old. Eight years later, after multiple severe bouts of the disease she became critically ill and was scheduled for intestinal surgery, but on preoperative investigation she was found to have, in addition to her ulcerative colitis, widespread Hodgkin's lymphoma. The symptoms of the lymphoma had been masked by her symptoms of colitis, a disease made worse by a poorly managed emotional status.

She died from the Hodgkin's before she could ever have surgery for the colitis. Had she not had colitis at all, or so many flares which required high dose immuno-suppressive medications which likely altered the time course and diagnosis of the Hodgkin's, perhaps she would be reading this today. But it was not to be. My mother was a sweet woman, and often festive, but as far as I am concerned, she literally worried herself to death. Rather than setting me off on a course of angst and despair, I took my mother's lesson well and doubled down on my conviction that emotional choice was critical.

Not long before the above-referenced events, I dropped out of college, moved out west, and worked to support myself. I became quite familiar with poverty and pain. Yet I also knew about freedom and responsibility. And all the while, I was choosing happiness.

Flash forward twenty-five years. At this point, I had now been living this way, purposefully and with awareness, for more than half my life. It was not fake. It was durable through trying times. I was having a discussion with friends—one a social worker, the other studying to be a social worker who also happened to be living with the diagnosis of major depression—about social work education, psychology and depression management, and philosophy in general. It was then that I first extensively elaborated my theory of Perspectivism, that happiness was a choice, and that we each as individuals had the power to choose for ourselves, in spite of circumstances around us, how we wanted to feel.

Immediately my friends encouraged me to codify these concepts. As social workers and people who used, first hand, and valued therapeutic tools to help people improve their emotional well-being and their lives in turn, they recognized the empowering potential of this simple construct.

So, encouraged, began this segment of the journey to share these ideas.

Why did I choose happiness to center my life on? In short, because it *felt* better. It still does. To me, and to those I was around. And happiness works, to boot!

I read Boswell's *Life of Johnson* when I was seventeen.[2] At one point in the tale, Samuel Johnson discovered a way to be a "good" man: he would keep a journal of his life and make sure the lead character—himself—would do the "right" thing as much as possible. Of course, he realized, this would require that in every moment of his life, he would have to keep in mind that he would be journaling about his actions later, and in so remembering he would be moved to behave nobly in the moment. For myself, if I wanted to be of any service to myself and my fellow travelers, I had to be the best "me" I could be, and that meant being happy. Fortunately, as it turns out, there is plentiful data now to support the notion that we can each be better for ourselves and better for all those around us by being happier.

Add to that, from a very early age I realized that it was easier to be happy when those around me were also happy. As the Wilcox poem goes: "Laugh, and the whole world laughs with you."[3] Or, at least, the reverse was true: it was harder to be happy when those around me were unhappy.

So it made sense that, if I wanted it to be easy to be happy, one of the best ways to go about it was to make other people happy. This doesn't, of course, contradict the notion that our own individual happiness comes, ultimately, from within ourselves. I am not saying that we can only be happy when those around us are as well. It is just that there are circumstances in which happiness is easier to attain and maintain.

So I decided to work on developing Practical Perspectivism as not just a philosophy, but as a constructive way to make my own world better by helping those around me find their own way to happiness. There seem to be so many books guiding people to achieve—wealth, love, power—as if those things lead to happiness. But we all know, instinctively and by a plethora of examples, that these things do not guarantee happiness.

Sure, just like having those around you being happy can create the circumstances in which it's *easier* to be happy, having money, love, and power can contribute to your circumstances making it easier to be happy, but not necessarily. And why is this true? Because, again, ultimately, happiness comes from within. In the end, it is independent of external factors.

It is a decision you must make, to be happy. It is a choice. No matter how "good" your situation in life is, there will always be things to be unhappy about if you choose to focus on them. And no matter how "bad" things are, there will always be something "good" to focus on to be happy about. You, and only you, can choose for yourself. Every moment, in every situation.

Many self-help books are perfectly fine at helping individuals achieve many of the things they claim—even perhaps transient happiness. But for lasting happiness you must recognize that your emotional state, your *happiness,* remains intrinsically determinable every moment, every day. Only a dedicated way of life can attain and maintain such a state. That is where Practical Perspectivism, as a philosophy, and as a guide back to your own self, comes into play.

Recently an acquaintance made an offhand comment about my behavior, claiming I had a need to be liked. I was intrigued by this, and looked at myself with a critical eye: do I have a *need* to be liked?

I asked myself this because I found I generally adopt an attitude with others—those I know, as well as those I don't—that I reliably expect will result in people liking me. I could act differently, but I choose not to. For example, this self-questioning came during a day when I was working in my day job as an anesthesiologist. I was teamed with an anesthesia resident and orthopedic surgeons I had never worked with before. I introduced myself to the surgeons, asked what they needed and what they expected, and requested that they not hesitate to communicate to me their intraoperative needs.

This is seemingly innocuous enough, but occurs far too infrequently in the medical world—understandably to some degree, I guess, since we are always trying to project an aura of supreme knowledge. Similarly with my resident—I made it clear to her that we would learn throughout the day, some things would go smoothly and some less so, but that we would maintain our focus on the larger picture of patient care, really the only thing that matters in our profession.

My resident was unsuccessful placing the first IV, and the second. I maintained an upbeat banter which relieved my resident, kept our patient feeling relaxed, and reassured the surgeons. I could have responded differently and everyone in the room would have had a less pleasant experience, especially the patient. We got our next IV placed and the case, and day, proceeded without further hitch.

I thought about why I want people to like me. I realized it was not necessarily simply a desire to be liked for my own sake, but rather such that when people see me coming, or know that they will be with me in any capacity, they will automatically be happier than they would if they *didn't* like me. And if those around me are happier, it makes my immediate world a happier place and an easier place for me to be happy. It is a very basic formula.

Martha Beck, a life coach and best-selling author, in an interview in the *New York Times* said, "Everything I've ever taught in terms of self-help boils down to this—I cannot believe people keep paying me to say this—if something feels really good for you, you might want to do it. And if it feels really horrible, you might want to consider not doing it."[4] Now, this isn't to say that *all* behavior that "makes you feel good" is necessarily healthy or beneficial, but the kernel of truth is certainly in there, and we will tease this apart going forward. Suffice to say, there are other fine reasons that have become apparent as well, as we'll see, but most notably perhaps is that we are simply better "us" when we are happy.

In the few years I've been contemplating, researching, and writing this book, more works by many others have come into existence touting the benefits of happiness with the common thread of focusing on the moment at hand, rather than the past or worrying about the future. (Sure, planning for the future is always sound policy, but it seems that one of the best ways to do so is by focusing on the present as well). All these works, in some way or another, seem to validate the tenets of Practical Perspectivism.

So, in the end, Practical Perspectivism can help most anyone achieve greater and/or more lasting happiness. This, in turn, makes my own world a happier place and an easier place for me in which to sustain my own happiness.

Hence, this guide.

# CHAPTER 3

# THE TEN PRECEPTS OF PRACTICAL PERSPECTIVISM

To engage Practical Perspectivism (PP) in your life as a tool to find and maintain happiness, it is helpful to recognize ten basic precepts. They are presented here in one version of a logical order, that is to say, this starts with addressing choice before happiness, since accepting that we can choose how we feel comes before choosing happiness per se, but in reality these are tenets rather than steps. All of the precepts are in play simultaneously for the Perspectivist.

Think of them as prayers if you have a religious background, a mantra to meditate on if you are Buddhist-leaning, or just some simple rules of living. Commit them to memory, internalize them as your second nature, take them on faith when necessary. These ideas will be expanded upon throughout this treatise, but what follows is the most basic "how to" phrasing of Practical Perspectivism.

# THE TEN PRECEPTS OF PRACTICAL PERSPECTIVISM

1. You must accept that you *choose* to do every single thing you do.

2. You must realize at every moment, in every situation, you choose your perspective.

3. No one perspective is more valid than any other; all claim some access to "truth".

4. Each moment of existence can be viewed from an infinite number of perspectives.

5. Your perspective is limited primarily by your imagination only.

6. You are always free to choose a new perspective and, with that, new feelings.

7. You must *want* to be generally happy and at peace.

8. You must *believe* that you *can* be generally happy and at peace.

9. You must *accept* that it is *ok* to be generally happy and at peace.

10. Only you are in control of, and responsible for, your choices.

### 1. You must accept that you *choose* to do every single thing you do.

In discussing choosing our actions, we are referring to one concept with two parts. In the first place, there are the things we do, say, or don't do or say, physically—our outward responses to life. Part two is how we feel about all the things we do and all those that are impacting us. Practical Perspectivism suggests that we choose our feelings just as much as we choose, say, when to lay off the curve ball, whether to flip the bird to the motorist who just cut you off, or what to have for lunch. And in fact, what we choose to feel about something is inextricably linked to, is intrinsically interwoven with, what we end up choosing to do about it, and vice versa.

See here how everything
lead up to this day
and it's just like any other day
that's ever been.
Sun goin' up and then
the sun it goin' down...[5]

—The Grateful Dead

Our world around us is happening 24/7. We are exposed to, bombarded with, and seek out an extraordinary array of information from all five of our obvious senses as well as a wide variety of physiochemical senses (barometric pressure, radiation, and electro-magnetism for example). We exist in a constant state of computational analysis of all this data, consciously and subconsciously, and we act—or react—continuously.

Sometimes it is more obvious that we are making choices. Sometimes we deliberate for a longer period of time, talk to people, take in more information, do some research, and then conscientiously choose a planned course of action. But even for the actions that we spend less time consciously considering, we still choose those responses, however ill- or un- considered they may be. Any action more than a spinal arc reflex, the literal knee-jerk reaction, requires regulation and coordination from the cortex of our brains, the place in which we think and choose. Even inaction is a choice. We simply cannot act (including acting by inaction—to hold our body or tongue in reserve) without *choosing* to do so.

Certainly, at all times, our choices are limited—that is, our availability of actions is limited. But we always have some choice of options, even if that choice is only between action and inaction. Sometimes we may find ourselves in difficult, or even unthinkable, situations, and it is hard to imagine that we chose them. If thieves have broken into your home and are threatening you and your family at gunpoint, it is hard to remember that you chose to be there. But all the events that led up to that moment: the alarm system you may or may not have bought, the neighborhood you decided to live in, the job that afforded you the lifestyle you are living (which perhaps makes you a target for robbery), the vacation you decided not to take that week which meant you were home instead of on a beach in Jamaica at this moment—all these choices put you in that position at that moment in time. Whether we thought about any of these things as choices or not doesn't change the actual fact that they were indeed, obviously, choices.

You are not to blame, in the common sense—you didn't make all those choices so that bloodthirsty villains would come calling. You didn't choose specifically to have criminals break into your home, but your choices put you there just the same.

How you respond is equally your choice, and simultaneously dependent on previous choices you've made. Did you buy a firearm or not? Did you pursue martial arts training? That your options may all be bad doesn't change the fact that you still have choices. You could fight and risk death, you could offer to open the safe and stave off further destruction of property, or you could freeze up and not do anything other than tremble in a corner.

Furthermore, how you choose to respond will definitively affect how you choose to feel about the event later. You could choose to open the safe and feel like an idiot later because the thieves may never have found the safe, or you can feel wise because if you denied its existence and they found it anyway they might have killed your children. You can choose to feel victimized and vulnerable and never get a good night's sleep again, or you can choose to feel empowered that you survived such a desperate situation, you acted decisively and appropriately, and you know you can get through such trying times.

It is reported that women in the Congo, who have suffered brutalities perhaps beyond compare in this century—war, rape, poverty, and hunger, often inflicted by family members forcibly turned against them—respond to their own freedom when peace comes, not with classic western post-traumatic stress disorder, not with judeo-christo-islamic eye-for-an-eye revenge-seeking, but with a desire to build a home, farm, and live a peaceful family life.[6] These are choices, both physical and emotional.

So while we may not specifically choose all the circumstances of every situation we find ourselves in, especially because we exist in a world of sentient creatures likewise choosing their own courses which invariably intersect in unpredictable ways with ours, the following two statements remain undeniable: 1) all of our own choices are contributory to our circumstances in some measurable way and therefore confer some self-responsibility; and, 2) we still, nonetheless, have complete domain over the choice of, and responsibility for, what we think of, and how we feel about, the circumstances, how we emotionally move forward from said circumstances, and what physical actions we take next. The Nietzschean perspectivist would agree this is a most logical interpretation.

Remember, though, Practical Perspectivism is not necessarily saying you *should* be happy all the time—though theoretically you could be. The theory recognizes that some of life's circumstances make it difficult to find, or at least readily apply, the happy perspective. What Practical Perspectivism *does* do is give you the tools to find your way back to happiness more quickly, and empowers you to do so for your own physical and mental health, as well as for your fellow traveler and Mother Earth.

## 2. You must realize at every moment, in every situation, you choose your perspective.

Choosing to act is certainly more concrete a notion than choosing your perspective. Willfully making our muscles move is something we can latch on to rather handily. What we think, however, and how we feel, and the perspective we have on something—well, it is understandable to be skeptical that we *choose* these things. They hardly seem like actions at first blush.

To see differently, is no small discipline and preparation of the intellect for its future "objectivity'—the latter understood...as the ability to control one's Pro and Con and to dispose of them, so that one knows how to employ a variety of perspectives and affective interpretations in the service of knowledge.[7]

—Friedrich Nietzsche

Let's start by looking at opinions. You might have an opinion about someone you've just met. Even easier, someone you are going to meet. You might already know some of their background, perhaps, where they are from or what they do with their lives, how old they are, maybe even someone else's opinion of them. But you do not know this person yet. You have not met them.

It is normal and common to put together your limited

information, to think about it in several ways, and then to formulate an opinion—even though you still do not really know this person at all. This is a clear example of choosing a perspective. We don't yet know this person so we have no real basis to truly *feel* a certain way about them. Clearly, they, themselves, have not given us any particular reason to feel one way or another about them. Instead, we choose a perspective. We could easily imagine an alternate story to fill in the blanks in our knowledge about this individual, ascribe to them different motives for that which we do know about them, and we would therefore hold another opinion of them.

Then, upon meeting this individual, we continue the process of choosing, revising our original chosen opinion based on the first hand information we have just garnered. Sure, there are some "gut" feelings we may have which we ascribe to the impression that person has made on us, but we still factor in all the rest we know about the individual and modify our "gut" feelings to formulate an overall opinion. We choose, at some level, which bits of information to make more important, and assign less value to other bits of information. This is us choosing perspectives. And consciously or not, we go through a similar process about all things in all instances.

A good friend is developing a prototype scooter. On his initial mock-up, he used wheels he had around the shop. His wife unexpectedly took the scooter out in rainy weather and the bearings in the wheels were ruined. His initial gut reaction was anger, but before he let himself vent his frustration he looked at the situation perspectively—and an additional truth presented itself: he knew he'd eventually need sealed bearings. This event pushed him to obtain a better component and *improve* his design. And, he avoided a fight with his wife—wins all around.

Practical Perspectivism teaches us to be more purposeful, less arbitrary, less at the whim of our gut and more at the guidance of our considerable cognitive abilities in order to take greater command of our lives, our actions, and our emotions. There is nothing necessarily wrong with living an emotionally-charged life more at the whims of nature, but if happiness is a goal, and if you can affect that, why would you not try? Certainly we do not go out of our way to eat foods we don't like; we choose instead to eat foods that please us. Choose your perspective as you would your dinner.

### 3. No one perspective is more valid than any other; all claim some access to "truth."

We are talking about two kinds of truth here: physical truth and philosophic truth. Electrons collide, footballers step out of bounds—these are the former truth. How we interpret what we think we see, and how we feel about it, these make up the latter.

One such time I left town and on my way back, at a point where the land was high and I could see the sea to my left and down the road a long ways, I suddenly felt I was in heaven. The spot was in fact no different from when I had passed it not long before, but my way of seeing it had changed.[8]

—Yann Martel

At least theoretically, and oft-times actually, the existence of an absolute in the former, the physical truth, can be commonly agreed upon—even when unanimity about what that truth actually is may not be achievable.

At this point, I should mention Heisenberg's Uncertainty Principle, which states that it's impossible to simultaneously know both *where* anything is and *how* it is moving, which arguably calls the "knowing" of any physical absolute into question. In quantum physics, "anything" is commonly considered to be a wave of energy, but since all matter is really energy in some form or another, we cannot be absolutely and completely certain of *any* physical representation of said energy. Still, for daily practical considerations, moving out of the way of a bus that your are reasonably confident is on the road in front of you and heading in your direction is probably a good idea, regardless of what Heisenberg may have to say about it.

For the latter type of truth, this philosophical or emotional one, at least from a Perspectivist standpoint, there are infinite permutations and therefore there cannot be a unique, solitary absolute. So when it comes to the practice of day-to-day living—given the lack of an overarching "this is how it is" (or ought to be)—we are allowed to be empowered to choose essentially whatever viewpoint we wish from which to operate.

Since all perspectives of actual occurrences are real—that is, they actually exist in the continuum of space and time—we can reasonably choose from the perspectives available to our imaginations. Now, this is not to say that we are equally validated in living in the world as we know it by acting on our chosen perspective if we choose perspectives that are *provably* false.

For example, no amount of telling yourself your keys are in your pocket at this very moment in time will make it true if, in "fact," your keys are on the nightstand upstairs. You could choose a perspective that imagines you could still start your car without your keys and you can get in your car, but you still would *not* be able to start it without the key! Therefore, your chosen perspective would not be equally validated. Instead, upon realizing that you have to go all the way upstairs to fetch your keys, your initial perspective may be to feel bothered that you have to walk all the way back up the stairs. But take a moment and choose to tell yourself instead, "Ah well, another golden opportunity to burn 10 more calories and buy myself an extra spoonful of ice cream for dessert!" and you might start "forgetting" your keys all the time.

Imagine we can all agree what a "stone" is: a solid chunk of inorganic matter measuring more than an inch across but less than 5 inches across (smaller might be considered a pebble, say, and larger would be a rock or a boulder). Now imagine both my hands are visibly empty—no pebble, no stone, no boulder. Perspectivism could not be used to justify another individual's actions of physically accosting me on the basis of a perceived fear *I* was about to accost *them* with the "stone" in my hand. It would not be a valid perspective because it was simply an act of imagination based on a provably false premise.

It is important to distinguish between "real"—the perspective that is perceived by an individual, and that which is "true"—a provable fact that would be agreed upon from effectively any perspective. While an individual's perspectives may be real, they are perspectives of thought or emotion, perspectives that cannot necessarily or easily lay equal claim to "truth" agreeable to most others.

Your "real" perspective, from a paranoid standpoint, might be that I have a stone in my hand, and no amount of telling you or showing you otherwise might dissuade you. That perspective is real—to you. Nonetheless, that perspective does not represent provable fact—truth—that which would be agreed upon by everyone else who looked into my empty hand.

In purely Nietzschean perspectivism, the only "truth" is the individualized perspective of the beholder, and no amount of "provability" is worth the oxygen or ink needed to describe it. But unfortunately, Nietzsche wasn't particularly interested in translating his brilliance on this subject into an application for living. Practical Perspectivism stops short of his beautiful philosophical reach to enable us to function in the actual world we inhabit with others. PP allows for simple physical "truths" to exist for practical purposes, even if they are changeable under different conditions.

On Earth, if we drop a stone it will fall because of gravity. Any other individual standing by watching this event will agree that the dropped stone fell to the ground. This is practical, physical truth. It's possible to entertain a perspective that the Earth rose up to meet the stone, but quantifiable measurements of the Earth in the cosmos will "prove" otherwise. It can be further argued that the entirety of the universe shifted to meet the stone so the observed measurements of the Earth in the cosmos is irrelevant, but as a practical matter we will accept this notion to be ridiculous. If many stones were all dropped, in different places but from the same height, at once, it would be difficult to explain the entirety of the universe moving in multiple directions simultaneously to have the Earth meet each at precisely the same moment.

However, if you let go of the same original stone while floating in space, all bets are off on what might be the agreed upon observable "truth." So "truth" under certain reproducible conditions may well be rendered arguable under different circumstances.

Still, that doesn't change the fact that for practical real world, real life, everyday situations—which account for the vast majority of our life circumstances—physical "truths" exist. All perspectives may be entertained, but some are provably false. We can think whatever we like, but we might actually be specifically wrong sometimes.

In the realm of emotions, however, there isn't such a clear cut set of right and wrong. Provability has little place in matters of emotion. We may have a sense of social tact that guides us in most situations—we generally do not laugh at funerals, we try to be joyous at births, for example. But we could easily imagine various subtleties of circumstances that would allow us to have alternate emotional responses to most common life events.

We think and feel differently about the death of someone like Osama bin Laden than we do about someone we know personally and love. Similarities to physical truth do exist—that is, the conditions matter (like gravity on

Earth vs. the vacuum of outer space)—but how we each *feel* about a given physical event, even if we may all agree on the specific manner in which it occurred, is subject to each of our own unique individual set of experiences interacting with our own unique individual genetic makeup, and ultimately how we then *choose* to feel from the myriad possibilities.

Practical Perspectivism induces us to choose both what we *think* about a situation and how we *feel* about it. Some may think it sad that a SEAL team killed Osama, but they may feel OK about it. Others may think it great that such an event occurred, but still feel sad about it. This is perhaps where Practical Perspectivism matters most: what we choose to think and feel about, and accordingly respond to, the events occurring around us.

All our background is, without question, contributory, but ultimately, if we believe we are mindful, sentient individuals with free will, these thoughts and feelings are our choice. And PP suggests we can willfully choose to focus those thoughts and feelings in a manner most conducive to our own happiness and well-being as a way to most meaningfully contribute to the happiness and well-being of our world.

Accordingly, even if we choose to act in a manner that may seem altruistic at first glance—acting in the present in a manner that appears to increase the happiness and/or well-being of others at our own expense—Practical Perspectivism enables us to recognize a perspective that deems a seemingly altruistic act as actually benefitting our*selves*—at least emotionally. And we know that our emotional state affects our physical state and our environment, so by choosing how we feel about our supposedly altruistic actions, we actually turn them into self-serving ones that simultaneously benefit the greater good.

## 4. Each moment of existence can be viewed from an infinite number of perspectives.

Imagine time standing still for a single moment. Then imagine a marble floating in space. Now imagine an old-style film movie camera floating around that marble, first very close, then further and further away. Imagine each frame of the movie that the camera takes. Each frame is like our different perspectives from different vantage points.

What is greater than something else is "great,"
Therefore there is nothing that is not "great."
What is smaller than something else is "small,"
Therefore there is nothing that is not "small."[9]

—Chuang Tzu

The whole notion of perspectives became crystal clear to me during an intramural football game back in medical school. I was playing defense, cornerback, and the guy I was covering caught a pass at the sideline. Both teams' reserve players were congregated on that same sideline, so there were plenty of opinions—and emotions—about what had occurred. Obviously, the question was whether or not the player caught the pass in bounds. Nonetheless, the variety of descriptions of how his feet came down, where exactly each foot was, whether or not he had possession of the ball at the time, may have exceeded the number of people viewing the play.

I, of course, felt like I had the best vantage point, being closest to the receiver, being beaten on the play, and focusing my vision on his feet in the hope that he was out of bounds, rendering the pass an incompletion. But his teammates argued I was biased, and that my version of the event could not be believed.

I realized then that numerous, perhaps an infinite number of, circumstances color our perceptions, and that multiple perspectives of things and events, each of them real in their own specific time and place, can exist simultaneously. This occurs despite the fact that a true *thing* exists, and each singular *event* actually occurs, exactly and only one way.

This scenario is much like the instant replay reviews becoming popular in sporting events. There are the players and coaches, each seeing the singular event occurring instantaneously in the moment from where they stand on the playing field. Then there are the referees, umpires, line judges, commentators. Finally, there are the tens of thousands of fans in the stadium and the millions of people watching on TV. Each of them has seen the singular event, which happened in only one very specific way, from their own point of view, or perspective.

The replay officials also saw the play occur live in real time, but they have the advantage of pulling up several additional camera angles to aid their decision. They can utilize reverse action, stop action, zoom, and slow motion.

Sometimes they have enough additional perspectives, all of them real, to overturn the call. Sometimes there is ample evidence to definitively support the play the way it was originally ruled.

Yet other times, even all those extra views and tools do not yield sufficient conclusive evidence to confirm or reverse the call of the official on the field. And so the play stands as called. Not definitively wrong or right, just the perspective of the pre-determined individual who was charged with making the initial call.

Now, this is the situation with ostensibly provable facts: the play happened exactly one way. Yet the myriad of perspectives are also true for the individuals (and machines) viewing the event from their respective positions. Similarly, with opinions, ethics, morals, beliefs—ideas which are far less amenable to singular proofs of validity or invalidity— the same myriad of perspectives, all true from the eye, or mind, of the beholder, are similarly existent.

Consider the classical notion of God. You do not even have to go so far as to compare the many perspectives on God, interpretations of God's motives, desires, laws, attributes that exist between different religions. You can simply look at the multiplicity of views of God within one religion, say Christianity. There are Baptists and Lutherans and Protestants and Roman Catholics and Greek Orthodox and Presbyterians and the list goes on. They all agree with the notion that there is one God. They all agree with the notion that Jesus Christ was the son of that God. There are many more minor areas where their beliefs intersect.

They would all call themselves, and maybe even each other, Christians. But there remain some fundamental differences in their perspectives on how their version of God should be interacted with, and how that God interacts with them. Each of these religious viewpoints grew out of some more primary philosophies, yet somewhere along the line, some thinker had the imagination to view the orthodoxy from a different perspective. And they had charisma enough, and facility enough with language, to develop a following. It wasn't a *new* perspective—not in the sense that it didn't *exist* before. It just hadn't been imagined, or verbalized in a clear, cogent enough way, by a forceful enough soul.

## 5. Your perspective is limited primarily by your imagination only.

If there are an infinite number of perspectives, then every subtle difference between perspectives can be imagined, as can their polar opposites and everything in between.

Once in a while
you can get shown the light
in the strangest of places
if you look at it right.[10]

—The Grateful Dead

It can be argued, practically speaking, that our imagination is not infinite, that it is limited by our experiences, but that would just be selling our imagination short. Imagination is really just that—envisioning that which is beyond one's experience. Given that it requires extrapolation from what one knows to imagine what is beyond one's knowledge, then one can extrapolate from there on ad infinitum. Once one frees their imagination, all perspectives become possible—and once all perspectives are possible, choice becomes imperative.

As described previously with the movie camera analogy, while all moments are, in themselves, unique, the perspectives from which they can be viewed are as infinite as the universe itself, limited only by our imagination.

We even know, just from our own experiences in life, that we often view the same thing differently over time. The passing of time puts us in a different place, not just physically, but emotionally and experientially as well. It puts all the trappings of the world around us in different juxtapositions such that we end up viewing the same thing in our past, or a very similar thing in the future, differently.

These different views existed all along; we simply either fail to think of them or fail to look for them. In order to look for them, we have to remember that they always exist. If we are not happy or satisfied with either the perspective we have at any given time, the way our current perspective is making us feel, or the results we are achieving with our current perspective, we can stretch our imagination to view our circumstances from any other perspective. And then we can determine whether we wish to choose any new way to view our world.

## 6. You are always free to choose a new perspective and, with that, new feelings.

All perspectives exist simultaneously, come with likely emotional states, and new ones can be chosen *at any time*. And as we saw in Precept 3, our emotional responses are entwined with the perspectives we choose to view the events in our lives.

I must die. Must I then die lamenting? I must be put in chains. Must I then also lament? I must go into exile. Does any man then hinder me from going with smiles and cheerfulness and contentment?[11]

—Epictetus

Choosing perspectives is *already* how we function. Sure, it's true we are all raised under a distinct set of circumstances—familial, societal, political, religious, financial, etc.—which shape our perspective-choosing *bias*, but at every moment in our lives we are melding all these biases in different amounts to come up with an attitude and approach to each unique circumstance we encounter. We donate to charity A but not to B. We buy brand X instead of Y. The very notion of free will demands that we choose our perspective, and hence from that perspective we act. We are no more *forced* to perceive an occurrence as good or bad, right or wrong, than we are forced donate to charity A or B, or none at all.

That most of our "choices" are, in fact, occurring nearly reflexively without very much conscious "thought" at all doesn't make the act of choosing any less true. As stated before, we simply cannot act without *choosing* to do so. And how we act, once we choose to do so, demands we've already chosen a perspective from which to act. That sometimes we find ourselves spending some, or even quite a bit of, time determining how we "feel" or what we "think" about something before we act on it only highlights the reality of what is going on inside of us at multiple levels for all behavior.

Certainly, sometimes our habitual or reflexive "gut" emotions seem to get ahead of our considered actions, but that does not mean we are required to persist with our "gut" reaction. Once we recognize that we choose our reactions, we are free to adjust our attitude.

If we are told the glass of red liquid across the room is a fine red wine being served for our tasting, our whole sensory milieu is geared up for this wonderful treat. When, upon approaching the glass, we find it instead to be filled with blood, we might at first be repulsed (and perhaps disappointed).

But we are no more required to be repulsed than we are required to actually drink the stuff just because we once thought it was a fine wine we might enjoy. We could just as easily choose to say, "Oh well, there is a glass of natural red liquid that just happens to be something I have no interest in drinking," and be done with the emotionally charged revulsion.

You might *say* you hate the sight of blood, but that is only because you say so, because you've told yourself that your whole life, and because it is socially acceptable to be repulsed by the sight of blood. It is not that there is something inherently repulsive about this natural occurring, extremely valuable, and potentially life-saving red liquid. When viewed from this perspective, you could easily choose to *feel* differently about a glassful of the stuff. Certainly, if you were injured, bleeding, and told that no blood was available to save your life—and then the ambulance showed up and the EMT raced over with several units of the stuff, you would surely *feel* quite relieved—not repulsed—at its very sight. It is just a matter of perspective.

Practical Perspectivism tells us that we are, indeed, free to develop any perspective we like *and* any emotional response to that perspective. While the general suggestion here is to use PP to improve happiness and well-being, this need not be your goal at any given moment. Yet that does not change the power of the principle. Everyone is equally free to choose whatever individual perspectives—weird, wild or boringly "normal"—and emotions they like.

A yardstick nonetheless remains: are you achieving your goal(s) with the perspective and emotion you have chosen, either intentionally or by default? If so, great. If not, recognize that this was a situation you chose, and that you can change it. If there is any caveat here, it is whether, (or how much), you are harming others by following your chosen perspective. Remember as well that your course of action may elicit undesired responses from others. The social pressure reflecting back upon your world in response to your behavior cannot be dissociated from your choice. You can choose to attempt to discredit or discount it, but it still exists and interacts with your own internal and external state.

Accordingly, it becomes readily apparent that you serve yourself best by acting in a manner that impacts others and your world most positively and least negatively. Second only to choosing your internal state, that is the best way to impact your own life most positively. This is where PP distinguishes itself most clearly from other ego-based philosophies such as the so-called self-serving Cult of the Individual, discussed in more detail later.

Being considered "normal," "phobic," "antisocial," or just plain "weird" because of your chosen responses in given situations matters only to how it impacts your own environment. Don't forget that the world around you can make it more or less challenging to attain and maintain your goals, so it's worth considering your environment when determining your viewpoints and the associated emotional responses you harbor and display. Still, in the end, it doesn't ultimately matter what others think of you, or how they impact you, *if* you are satisfied with your status as is.

Having made that last declaration, you may question a belief system that seems to suggest it is OK for even the perverted mind to unabashedly, even happily, pursue its perversions regardless of how those pursuits may impact others. The issue of pathologic behavior is dealt with more thoroughly in Chapter 6, but for now it will be enough to make two observations. First, antisocialists already behave the way they behave, perhaps choosing to do so, or simply succumbing to diseases of the brain, despite society's disapproval of their behavior. Perverts do not currently utilize, nor do they need, PP to "justify" or condone their actions. Second, while PP elucidates why their thinking is short-sighted (as is any use of the philosophy to defend their choices), their actions—if in fact chosen consciously for the satisfaction they bring in the short term—will most likely result in consequences they would ultimately rather not suffer (jail, isolation, retribution). Their perverted house of cards will eventually fall down around them.

Still, at the risk of opening a moral can of worms somewhat outside the scope of this discourse, morality is a human construct. Sure, we mostly choose to agree upon some basics, but even that is somewhat arguable. Beyond a handful of commonly held ethics, cultures across the planet, even segments of society within one nation, often hold varied moral values. Suffice to say, the universe has no such illusions of any absolute morality.

It is also important to remember that choosing happiness does not require dispensing with empathy or denying sadness, sorrow, anger, regret. It is more a question of how long you want to spend experiencing those feelings, how long do you want to allow those emotions to dominate your life, your demeanor, define you?

PP allows us to be empathetic as well as emotional, but also to choose a path of happiness or peacefulness to deal with any situation any time you wish. Our innate ability to look at any situation from a variety of viewpoints, to "see something from someone else's point of view," is what gives us our ability to be empathetic in the first place. We can envision any number of emotional responses to any situation we may see others face and, with all these choices at our disposal, select which ones to apply to any situation we find ourselves in.

Our immediate reaction to a personal loss (like the death of a parent) or a world catastrophe (like the 2010 earthquake in Haiti or the 2004 Indonesian tsunami) might be one of sorrow or emotional upheaval. But we can accept those intense emotional reactions while at the same time choosing any number of other positive aspects to embrace. For example, perhaps that parent lived a long time and didn't suffer in dying, so there can be a rejoicing of a life well-lived. Or in the case of the catastrophe, you might take solace in the fact that your own family is safe from earthquakes and tsunamis, and that you can send aid of some sort to the victims.

Clearly we do not allow every tragedy to consume our lives forever. Eventually, and humans in general have a very strong inner compass for this that we can tap, we find our way back to normalcy. Perspectivism allows us to shorten that time interval to one of our own choosing. PP empowers us to imagine how we will feel when we have recovered from the blow, and then allows us to focus on that set of emotions, to let that feeling fill us in the present.

## 7. You must *want* to be generally happy and at peace.

No therapy, medicine, program, diet, or philosophy can ultimately work if we don't *want* it to work, nor will it keep working well if we do not continue to be rigorous with the plan.

You can't always get what you want,
but if you try sometimes,
you might find,
you get what you need.[12]

—The Rolling Stones

Dr. John Arden, psychologist and author, is a Director of Training in Mental Health for a large health care system in Northern California, overseeing programs in 24 medical centers with over 100 postdoctoral residents and interns yearly. Dr. Arden also provides counseling, and presents workshops on brain-based therapy worldwide. He writes eloquently of a FEED program, with Focus (F) and Effort (E) being the starting points as a means of re-wiring our brains:

> You need to pay attention to the situation [Focus], the new behavior, or the memory that you want to repeat or remember. Attention activates your frontal lobes, which ensure that other parts of the brain are

> engaged...Effort shifts your attention from perception
> to action. Making focused effort activates your brain
> to establish new synaptic connections.[13]

One could say that it is like riding a bicycle. Before you knew how to ride, it seemed hard. When you were learning to ride, it was hard, but you stuck with it. Like so many things, the more you did it, the easier it got. Finally, now, whenever you get on a bicycle, you can ride. Sure, you may be a little wobbly for the first couple of minutes if it's been a few years, but in no time at all, really, you'll be racing around corners.

Learning to be happy, and to stay happy, is not so different. Once you train your mind to seek happy and peaceful perspectives, once you remember to look for them whenever you get caught up in other disturbing, depressing matters that are taking you away from your happy center, it is easy to re-stabilize yourself. And once re-stabilized, you can always revisit whatever issue was troubling you but from a much more rational, and likely more productive, place.

Furthermore, emerging neuroplasticity data tells us the more we exercise the connections which lead us to, or sustain us in, happiness, the more we inhibit those neural pathways that lead us down our dark alleys.

Neuroplasticity describes the ability of the brain to persistently modify its connections, strengthening some neural pathways, weakening others. There may even be some ability to generate new neurons and create new synapses between neurons in our brains that didn't exist before. Where once upon a time in the not so distant past scientists believed that the brain was static and could not really grow or change, we have now learned that our brains are "plastic," that is, they can be remodeled, albeit with mindful effort, behavioral modifications, and physical or environmental changes. After a fashion, we rewire our brains to self-fulfill our desires.

It would be somewhat unfair, of course, not to note that truly chemically imbalanced individuals may obviously be more challenged in changing their brain function. Still, even this remains somewhat dependent on degree, as data from Cognitive Behavioral Therapy (CBT) practice suggests (more on this in Chapter 7).

Really, it is a matter of deciding what type of person you want to be: a happy person who might, at times, experience sorrow, anger, etc., or a sad/angry person who occasionally experiences happiness. Or something in between: a person who is simply alive, experiencing both joy and sorrow as they come and go.

There will always be roadblocks in your way. There will always be many things you want. But if happiness is preeminent, admit it, embrace it, and the obstacles fall away. The other desires take a supporting role. Ultimately, you will find most of your other desires easier to obtain, or the failure to obtain them much easier to abide, than if you predicate your happiness upon having or achieving those other things.

## CHOOSE HAPPINESS!

Happiness must be its own goal. Many circumstances can make it easier to attain, but nothing else can, in the end, bring it to you. To be happy (or happy more often), you must *want* to be happy.

## 8. You must *believe* that you *can* be generally happy and at peace.

We actually have to be *willing* to succeed at making our lives happier, our roads smoother, and have faith that such success is blatantly achievable.

The function of prayer is not to influence God,
but rather to change the nature of the one
who prays.[14]

—Soren Kierkegaard

I said and said and said these words,
I said them, but I lied them.[15]

—Dr. Seuss

As the quote from Dr. Seuss's "What Was I Scared Of?" suggests, simply telling yourself over and again that something is true doesn't necessarily make it true. But this objection applies primarily to more easily definable "facts" and less so, maybe not at all, to emotions. In the realm of emotions, telling yourself to feel a certain way may not make a palpable difference at first, but neuroscientific data suggests that it *does* work over time, that pathways in the brain are laid down and reinforced with repetition, strengthening the used pathways and weakening the unused ones, as noted. Eventually, when it comes to the way your brain and your emotions work, telling yourself something over and again actually *can* help make it so. But it really helps to truly believe it, invest yourself, give yourself over to it, and not think of it as lying to yourself.

Emotions are far more malleable than "facts," far more subject to subtle changes based on constantly refreshing databases than are facts. In just this way, Seuss' character in "What was I scared of..." ultimately was *only* able to change his perspective as new information came available. The pants he'd been so terrified of were still, "pants with nobody inside them"—they hadn't changed— but when he learned that they were just as scared of him as he was of them, a commonality was found that allowed him to overcome his own fear. He would have saved himself so much angst, avoided so much cardiac and gastrointestinal stress, and achieved a productive relationship with those pants so much quicker if only he *believed* what he told himself over and over again—to choose the perspective and *believe* it, instead of *believing* he was lying to himself.

Practical Perspectivism reminds us to be cognizant of the simple fact that we are our own source of database refreshment—that we can, and in fact already do, determine our own emotional state. By seeking alternative perspectives, we can gain insights, viewpoints that allay our sadnesses and make it easier to find our way back to happiness and peacefulness.

Certainly we are all familiar with achieving some degree of "attitude adjustment" in the first place. Whenever we engage in something that "takes our mind off" of a particular item we'd prefer to not think about, we are engaging in Practical Perspectivism, shifting perspectives to manipulate our emotional state. PP, practiced as an ongoing process, achieves meaningful "truth" in every possible way by preventing moments of alternative negative emotional morass to take up long term residence. Making perspective adjustments becomes self-reinforcing and essentially reflexive.

In turn, we come to realize if we want to be happy, and we can be happy, it is really just a matter of whether or not we want to put in the effort required to be happy. And in the end, we realize it is not so much effort at all, just a matter of being mindful of our own role in our emotional state. Furthermore, after a time, you will find that it is far easier to remain conscious and disciplined with respect to your feelings than it is to always be buffeted about by the swirling winds of emotional instability. This is Arden's second E of FEED: effortlessness; as he writes, "Your brain won't have to work as hard once you reach this level."[16] (The D is for Determination, and serves as a basis for Dr. Arden's whole concept.)

## 9. You must *accept* that it is *ok* to be generally happy and at peace.

The universe doesn't care from which perspective any given individual chooses to view any moment.

That should be all the license anyone needs to be happy, if that is their desire. Really, it's OK—nobody (all right, very few) will take issue with anyone who has found a way to be happy, any time, any where. Sure, they may be *jealous*, but that's on *them*.

**Nothing brings down walls as surely as acceptance.**[17]

—Deepak Chopra

Obviously, this precept is much easier to understand and accept from the atheist's perspective, where there is no self-aware, self-motivated super-entity like a monotheistic God that might indeed *care* how individuals act. If the universe is incapable of judgment or free will, and there is no other omniscient, omnipotent entity to intervene, then certainly the individual is free to choose any practical, imaginable perspective. Nonetheless, this can also be accepted with ease within a religious belief system.

The religious soul is quite familiar with the notion of faith: the ability to believe something to be true that may defy standard scientific method proofs of such. It is a short leap from there to have faith that your chosen god, a god as worthy of one's faith as one may try to be of such a god's love and mercy, wishes us all to find peace and happiness, as is professed in some way or another and at some time by most religious interpretations. And it is a short leap from *there* to have faith that such a worthy god, while perhaps prescribing and proscribing certain behavioral "norms," would still respect each individual's perspective choices *within* those rather broad confines.

Given the plethora of interpretations of the western God's word, and given the belief that this God *gave* us this illimitable capacity to think, to imagine, it is entirely reasonable for a person of religious faith to have faith that God is prepared for us, perhaps even *expects* us, to choose practical perspectives that can bring our souls to a more peaceful place. This is especially true when we consider sociologic research that consistently shows happy people tend to be more compassionate, charitable, and willing to aid their fellow humans. Given that these are all traits encouraged by organized religions in the name of God, the God-fearing may well be convinced that it is their mandate *from* God to choose to be happy.

However, whether theist or atheist, Practical Perspectivism's notion that the *universe* doesn't care what you choose doesn't mean that *you* shouldn't care. Quite the contrary, your choice of perspective, and action, is critical to your experience of life, and directly impacts the people and events around you. Accordingly, you should care intensely, and should therefore take the utmost consideration, consciously, in those choices.

## 10. Only you are in control of, and responsible for, your choices.

Every action you choose affects everything around you, even if a direct link is not immediately obvious. This is a corollary of the Butterfly Effect, a term coined by physicist Edward Lorenz in the early 1960s to describe the notion that a butterfly flapping its wings in one part of the planet could theoretically affect the formation of a tornado somewhere else on the planet at some later point in time. Similarly, everything that occurs around us, near and far, and ever has occurred, to affect the quantum nature of our immediate universe at any given moment in time also affects our perspective and is implicated in helping to shape our choices. Nonetheless, far from abdicating free will, this concept allows us to recognize that even though there are an infinite number of factors (which are theoretically determinable, but practically not so) affecting our decisions at any moment, we are free to choose which we wish to allow to prominently influence our decision for a choice of action.

We stand at the crossroads, each minute, each hour, each day, making choices. We choose the thoughts we allow ourselves to think, the passions we allow ourselves to feel, and the actions we allow ourselves to perform. Each choice is made in the context of whatever value system we have selected to govern our lives. In selecting that value system, we are, in a very real way, making the most important choice we will ever make. Since the foundation of all happiness is thinking rightly, and since correct action is dependent on correct opinion, we cannot be too careful in choosing the value system we allow to govern our thoughts and actions.[18]

—Benjamin Franklin

While neuroscience confirms that our brain affects our mind, perhaps in ways we remain less than immediately aware of, it has also confirmed that our mind affects our brain. That is to say, how we feel, and what we think, affects the way our brain operates. It's a two-way street. And with purposeful effort, focus, and control of our mind, we gain greater awareness and mastery of our own emotional state and our own actions. Furthermore, in our choosing of any particular action, we are compelled to recognize and accept the consequences of those actions.

Simply put, recognizing we are always in the position of choosing our actions demands a few other admissions. First, as individuals, we are each the sole, final source of the choices we make, no matter how many sources we consider. Second, we are consequently responsible for the choices we make, the actions we take, and the effects those actions have on ourselves and others. Sure, the range of the possible choices and possible effects is mind-boggling. But that doesn't change the nature of the responsibility, or absolve us from trying our best.

# CHAPTER 4

# THE PERSPECTIVIST LIFE

Ok. So let's agree for the moment that if we *could* be happy—that is, if we really could choose, at any moment to be happy or not happy—we'd prefer to be happy. How can we actually live life this way?

It certainly seems, in most circumstances, a large swath of humanity is seeking something akin to happiness, or at least seeking to be happier than they are. Throughout this book, reasons and benefits as to why this is so are regularly cited, including health, general productivity, and the common good. We recognize that, in general, our common goal on a daily basis and in the long run is to attain, and maintain, happiness. We certainly don't routinely make conscious choices, all things being equal, to be unhappy. Even if we must make difficult choices, choices we may rather not have to be in a position to be making, we usually strive to make the choice that we hope will lead to the least bad, or best possible, outcome. This is all Perspectivism at play.

And in the end, the love you take
is equal to the love you make.[19]

—The Beatles

One could question: why happiness? Is happiness important? Is it a virtue, or even good? Sure, there are definable health and productivity issues, and the Perspectivist generally believes living a basically happy life approaches the level of something akin to a moral imperative—but it is not the argument here that there is necessarily some inherent "good" in happiness. There may or may not be, but that is certainly a separate question. The point is that people seem to live life seeking happiness, trying to be happy, or at least happier. For better or worse. And if that, at least, is true, Practical Perspectivism provides a road map.

We already live Perspectivist lives to a degree, whether we recognize it or not. And since we are already living this way albeit perhaps below or beyond our level of awareness, it's really a very small step to live this way consciously and gain every possible advantage from doing so. The advantages to be gained are many, including greater happiness, less guilt, less stress, and—just maybe—healthier and longer lives as a result.

The first step to living this way, consciously, is to keep in mind the ten basic precepts, worth paraphrasing here:

> Every moment of existence can be viewed from an infinite number of perspectives which are limited only by your imagination and all of which contain some validity, even if only internally. You choose your perspectives and everything you do—and you can always change your choices. Only you are responsible for your perspectives, your choices, and your actions.

It is also critical to remember that everyone else, whether they are aware of it or not, whether purposefully or not, is living their own Perspectivist life. Which is to say that you are not ultimately responsible for *their* choices or their feelings—their perspectives. Now, this is *not* to say that nothing you do *affects* anything or anyone else. Quite the contrary. *Everything* affects everything. In an energy-connected universe, we can't escape our oneness, our interconnectedness. But in the end, we each determine our perspectives inside our own minds, and are thus responsible for them. And just as you can create environments for yourself in which it is easier to be happy, you can create environments in which it is easier for others to be happy as well. Or more difficult.

The reality is we cannot possibly be responsible for the choices others make, since—especially in a Nietzschean sense (see Chapter 8)—their perspective is derived exclusively from within their own brain. Forget about undermining *their* responsibility, we would be undermining one of the main pillars of our philosophy that puts us in the position of being, ultimately, solely responsible for our own choices. If we are responsible for another's, or by extension everyone's, choices, then everyone else is responsible for ours and before you know it we've abdicated free will and sovereignty of self. Clearly, little could be more contrary, even anathematic, to the Perspectivist.

A close friend, one of my oldest friends here in New York City, a cancer survivor who's weathered her share of tsouris (Yiddish for troubles and bad times), lives down in Greenwich Village, with what used to be a clear view of the Twin Towers before they were knocked down. She was in the fortunate position of being able to accommodate friends as they fled the scene. Seeing the smoke rising from the smoldering buildings impacted her severely—yes, she is a very sensitive soul who takes everything to heart, but this was a big one for sure.

While she remained reasonably functional over the next several weeks in her job, she nonetheless spun into a bit of a depression. Every morning, walking to work past the view of the now missing towers, this deep-seated funk was reinforced.

Then one morning, upon passing that viewpoint again, she stopped herself, recognized what she had become since 9/11, and decided to make a choice. She would overcome her depression. Simple as that. She realized she could choose—that the events had occurred, and they were horrible, but she could either extend the horror by letting them diminish her every day, or she could mitigate the horror by actively choosing to brighten her outlook, to look to the future instead of dwelling on the past, and to continue her work of improving people's everyday lives through her work with gusto. She recognized her existing perspective was draining her, diminishing her work and creativity, and worsening the effect of the terrorist attack, and she *chose* to change her perspective—and it made a difference immediately.

She also recently related to me the advice of a Yoga teacher she sometimes studies with who routinely, in short refocusing breaks between particularly vigorous sessions, reminds his class to focus on what they *have*, what they *can* do, instead of what they do not have or cannot do. Anyone who has ever attempted any form of organized physical activity is certainly familiar with the obvious (the Michael Jordans and Wayne Gretzkys excepted): there's always someone out there, perhaps the person next to you on the mat or the field, who can throw farther, run faster, or hold the position longer. Sure, thinking about how we perform in comparison can serve as a motivator, but it's a double-edged sword in that it can allow self-doubt and frustration to infiltrate and potentially compromise our own ability and performance. Conversely, simply focusing on the attributes we do have and how we can work to improve those traits serves the same purpose without the potential downside. Two perspectives of the same perfect imperfections.

Another important aspect of living a Perspectivist life is understanding a bit about how others behave. People are not one-dimensional. We know this to be true just by looking inside our own selves again. Yet we often find ourselves ascribing one-dimensional reasoning to others' actions, particularly those that impact us. We think, "She said that to me because…" she likes me/hates me/wants to piss me off/wants something from me. In truth, however, it is invariably a complex balancing act between subtleties of emotions, perspectives, options, and reasoning that lead us to our *own* observed behaviors. No less is true for our co-

conspirators in life. We know how difficult it is to track all the things that go into our own decisions—how much more so, therefore, is it to know what mysterious set of circumstances leads another to their behavior?

Recognizing the complexity of our counterparts can help us understand them a little bit better, if only for giving us the ability to assign the notion of complexity as an explanation for those behaviors that are "beyond" us, or conversely, seem overtly simplistic. And this understanding can go a long way in affecting our own perspective in judging them.

Commonly this will end up softening our indictments, or, even better, deterring us from passing judgment in the first place. Remembering to "walk a mile in their shoes" as it were, helps us see the world as others see it. Understanding where other people *might* be coming from, even if we can't *precisely* visualize their perspective, enables us to adjust our own perspective accordingly and perhaps with greater tolerance. Because after all, the greater understanding we have of the world and the people around us, the better equipped we are to adopt wiser, more productive, happiness-producing perspectives ourselves.

## The Happiness Mantra

Madeleine L'Engle wrote, in my humble opinion, one of the greatest books ever, *A Wrinkle in Time.*[20] I read it when I was around nine years old, but it wasn't until I was sixteen that I really made use of it. And when I did so, I'm not really at all sure I recognized that my actions were echoing what the protagonist, Charles Wallace, did in the book.

In order to avoid being taken over by IT, a telepathic super-brain that controlled the population of Camazotz, Charles Wallace and his friends recited nursery rhymes in their heads. I was sixteen and in the midst of having a moment of psychological crisis when I recognized it was the constant re-playing of past and future social scenarios in my head, an incessant self-critiquing of how I *should* have behaved instead of how I *had*; it was this chronic habit of trying to play out every possible scenario and pitfall in the hope of avoiding it that was driving my anguish in the first place. Psychologist Julie Norem refers to this style of behavior, elaborated on later, as "defensive pessimism,"[21] and suggests that embracing it helps such thinkers perform better. All it did was overwhelm me with angst, leaving me dysfunctional and incapable of dealing with the present adequately.

I decided I simply had to stop thinking that way. I needed to learn how to nip those thoughts in the bud, as it were. And that is when the thought came to me of reciting nursery rhymes whenever I realized I was starting to spin "What ifs…" in my head. It worked like a charm.

Admittedly, it's a little like doing what every toddler does when they want to tune something out: stick your fingers in your ears and say "la-la-la-la…" Sometimes it takes that sort of effort to stop negative thoughts, but that's OK.

The nursery rhymes—or the la-la-la's, or whatever you find you can rely on—become, in effect, like a mantra for meditation. They function as a mental focusing vehicle. Find something simple that works for you. In all likelihood, you will find you only need to rely on your mantra for a short while. Once you reset your way of thinking, it tends to stay reset even without the mantra. You will soon find yourself simply thinking differently. Sure, every once in a while you may be particularly challenged in finding your way to a happy perspective, and then your mantra will be a good guide back. But for the most part, once you learn to activate your mantra immediately whenever you are otherwise inclined to wallow in disturbing trivialia, and to look instead for your happy place, you begin to do so reflexively, bypassing both the enticement and the need of the mantra.

In a similar fashion, and in addition to a happiness mantra in your head that you can carry around everywhere and is accessible at any moment in any situation, many people describe happiness-inducing activities they routinely rely on. For example, in an interview with Gretchen Rubin for her fantastic Happiness Project blog, Jonah Lehrer, a best-selling author who has written about creativity and happiness in several of his many fascinating books, notes that simply walking—setting aside what he is doing when it stumps him or otherwise bogs him down—works quite well for him.

"While I used to assume that my walks were a form of procrastination," says Lehrer, "I now see them as part of my work day. They make me happy, which is an ideal mental state for moments of insight."[22]

Any activity, memory, event, or even an object can serve as such a transportation device—an amulet if you will—reminding us of the happy place we really want to exist in.

Several years ago, when I first started writing about Practical Perspectivism, I was nearing the end of a leave of absence and contemplating my return to work. I was travelling with my family and friends. We were on the last day of our ten-day journey through the Italian Alps and the Cinque Terre along the Ligurian Sea. We were finally at a naturalist beach that we'd been pursuing for a couple of days, and I was lazily and happily floating in my birthday suit on the blue, blue Ligurian Sea looking up at an equally blue sky over the charming and picturesque ancient town of Corneglia. "It certainly doesn't get much better than this," I thought to myself. I burned that view, that scene, deep into my memory banks, actively making as many neural connections as possible. I was thinking ahead to the long cold late night shifts I'd be working in the hospital in a few months and how I would be thus able to bring back to mind at will this particular moment, memory, feeling. As it turns out, just writing about it brings back that feeling. And certainly, as often as I've needed in the years since, I have called on that memory to great satisfaction, both late at night in the hospital and in many other potentially stressful situations. Pleasure, and "flow" (more later), and meaning all rolled into one—and derived from nothing more than languidly luxuriating bare bottomed in the sea—for surely that which makes me a happier, less-stressed individual, also makes me better a physician for my patients.

## Grooks

> The universe may
> Be as great as they say
> But it wouldn't be missed
> If it didn't exist. [23]

—*Megalomania*, Piet Hein

How's that for ultimate perspective! Like many such adages, they are obvious once we hear them, but we may never before have actually thought about the point they are making.

Piet Hein, a Dutch mathematician-writer-inventor-philosopher, wrote a series of books called *Grooks*, filled with aphorisms, witticisms, and some of the most concise statements of Perspectivism I've ever come across (though Mr. Hein never classified them as such himself). Sure, Taoist writings may be more well-known examples of perspectivist thought, and Nietzsche more readily referenced, but Piet Hein's simplicity remains unsurpassed.

I began my relationship with *Grooks* years ago, but only recently, in the writing of Practical Perspectivism, did I come to realize how influential they were to me in developing Perspectivist thought for myself. I was in my mid-teens, writing poetry, when I was given two *Grooks* books for my birthday. Several of the short poems have lived with me ever since, and I have passed their simple wisdom on to many others. My daughter has been able to recite several of them almost since she was able to speak.

It ought to be plain
How little we gain
By getting excited and vexed;
We'll always be late
For the previous train
And always in time for the next. [24]

   *—Thoughts on a Subway Platform,* Piet Hein

Elegant. The notion contained herein applies to all sorts of circumstances. It teaches us not to lament the past or things we've missed; we cannot change any of it (if one accepts a linear nature of time, of course). Yet if we fail to remember to be present in the present, we may very well miss the next boat as it comes to our shores.

We use the terms "charmed" and "cursed" to describe people's luck in life. But do we really believe in charms or curses? Probably not. What we are observing instead is people who live in the present, who remember to "be here now" as Ram Dass exhorted, and who are therefore always ready to take advantage of the ride on the next train. These are the people who live "charmed" lives. It is not white magic. Nor is it a black cloud that afflicts the "cursed," but a dwelling on the past, or future even, and the concomitant missed opportunities for joy in the present. These people tend to focus on the difficulties that have befallen them or the problems they believe they are bound to encounter tomorrow.

A ski instructor once coached my wife not to look at the people down the slope, even though she was afraid of running into them. He said she was more likely to hit them by focusing on trying to avoid them than by just skiing. What is true on skis is even more so in life at large. If we focus on the past, we will keep bumping into the same difficulties; if we focus on future problems we will more likely lead ourselves directly to them.

But if instead we practice Practical Perspectivism at a conscious level, if we pay attention to the ever-changing present, we will be able to deal with what is here and now in a current and appropriate fashion leaving us feeling more exhilarated than fatigued, more able to move right or left as necessary to avoid danger, conflict, as desired. It is not a matter of ignoring or suppressing our past, but of applying our past experiences in a considered manner, in real time, to our current ones, learning from our mistakes instead of repeating them.

I was once told that when walking on ice, move at the speed at which you would fall. At first glance, this may seem a dangerous proposition, but if you think it through, the sense becomes clear. If you move too slowly and slip, your legs will be unprepared to stay under you and keep you up. If you move too quickly and slip, your body's inertia will keep it moving quickly while your legs suddenly lose traction and the ability to stay under you. But if you move at the speed at which you would fall, then your whole body moves together. If you slip, your legs stay under you, and you have the best chance of maintaining or regaining your balance. Moving through the emotional landscape of life, a tricky proposition at best, is more than just a little bit like walking on ice.

If a nasty jagged stone
Gets into your shoe
Just be glad it came alone
What if it were two? [25]

—*Stone in Shoe,* Piet Hein

Sometimes we forget that circumstances cannot be other than how they are—if they could have been otherwise they would have been so, and if we want them to be otherwise we must actively strive to make them so. Often, instead, we find ourselves focusing on how our circumstances could be better, no matter how good they might be at the moment. Now this is not necessarily a counterproductive exercise, as long as we continuously bear in mind how fine circumstances currently are. The first step in this exercise is maintaining a healthy respect for the possibility that circumstances could always be worse. This may be more important even than the pursuit of "better" circumstances, since it encourages us to recognize the existing positive aspects of our situation. As "Stone in Shoe" so simply reminds us, things can always be worse. And since this is true, it means that whatever circumstances you do find yourself in are better than other possibilities. Don't throw that away.

To be brave is to behave
Bravely when your heart is faint,
So you can be really brave
Only when you really ain't. [26]

—*Brave,* Piet Hein

Even when circumstances are difficult, trying, fear-inspiring, there still remain perspectives with which we can bolster ourselves to be courageous. While happiness might not be the emotion of the moment, neither will dread rule. Your actions will proceed from a place of power, such that when the situation abates, you will be able to return to happiness more quickly, feeling good about how you went forward in that situation, whether or not things turned out well.

I have since acquired several more Grooks books over the years, but Volume II, one of my first, remains my favorite, with many fine commentaries on Perspectivist living.

## Bit by Bit

It's hard to imagine what this type of life feels like. I could tell you it feels really good, but that probably doesn't help much. Fortunately, it doesn't really matter much either. If you harbor a nagging feeling there must be a better way, you'll likely be willing to try living Perspectively.

> Sure don't know what I'm goin' for
> but I'm gonna go for it for sure. [27]
>
> —John Perry Barlow

As the lyric says, sometimes you just have to go for it. Most of the time, we have no exact idea of how things will be in the future. Yes, we can make educated guesses as discussed earlier, and that's an important part of guiding our current actions, but we don't *know* with certainty. That's all right. In recognizing that, since we *cannot* know the exact vector and strength of every bit of energy in the universe at any given moment and as such we *cannot* know the future with absolute certainty, it becomes a bit easier to give up the feeling of *needing* to know.

What *is* important in thinking of the future is imagining how you might feel in the future if things you are doing now actually work out well. Or if you are currently experiencing hard times, imagine what it will feel like in the future when you have recovered from those hard times. You can also remember what it was like when you've recovered from hard times in the past and then imagine feeling that way now.

From all we've learned about neuroplasticity, we

know that just thinking things like this helps us actually feel these things in real time. Not fake feelings, but real, neurologically discernible positive emotional states. And the more we think this way, the more we curb the otherwise overactive negativity that can depress us and similarly build itself up while suppressing positive emotion.

From child psychology we know that negative labeling of children can engender more of the very behavior we may wish to see them overcome. This is no less true for ourselves as adults. Similarly, if you wish to be happy, you must stop telling yourself that you cannot be, or you don't deserve to be.

Yet labeling can have a positive component. It is not that we should be telling ourselves things that are provably false—it would do me little good to tell myself I am the strongest man in the world. However, I can think of myself as "strong"—as Chuang Tzu might say, there is nothing that is not stronger than something else, therefore there is nothing that is not strong. We must allow every possible moment of happiness to engulf us, to be that happy person. Only then will that label begin to fit.

Gretchen Rubin, author of *The Happiness Project*,[28] mentioned earlier for her wonderful blog, has set up Happiness Project groups across the country. She lived a prototypical western life, ripe for Practical Perspectivism:

leading a successful professional career with two healthy children and a loving spouse. She knew she had much for which to be grateful. And she *was* more or less happy. But she felt, she *knew*, she could be happier, and happy more often.

She set out to design a Happiness Project for herself, dedicating each month of one year to a different aspect of her life that she would focus on improving, adding the new concept each month while trying to maintain her growth in the previous month's category. Her months had themes like boost energy, remember love, aim higher, and lighten up. And she knew that every individual's own happiness project would be different, as we are all unique with our own strengths and weaknesses.

Ms. Rubin's approach is an excellent one—we could all benefit from working on our weaknesses. And it works. She is happier than she was. It has practical applications, but it is also just not quite a fundamental unifying philosophy, like Practical Perspectivism, and so it will commonly still fall somewhat short in bringing longer-lasting, more easily recoverable happiness. Ms. Rubin makes note of this herself. Still, anything that effectively works as a doorway to more happiness is a fine start down the road of living a Perspectivist life.

The Jim Carey movie, *Yes Man*, related a common point about philosophical applications: early on in the adoption phase of a new regimen (we even see this with practical pursuits like diets and exercise regimens), it is important to perform the functions "religiously"—that is, with dogged determination in all things. In *Yes Man*, Carey's character had to say "yes" to everything instead of "no" to the many requests he usually did. From this behavior, good things would come, he was assured. And so they did. But he was also told, initially, that bad things would happen if he didn't follow the rule. And so he became superstitiously afraid, and incapable, of saying "no."

Ultimately he did feel compelled to say no to something, and when bad things did follow he sought out the movement's guru who enlightened him: You don't have to say "yes" always forever, just to get started, to change your habits. Of course you must use common sense in making choices the remainder of your life!

With Practical Perspectivism, applying the happy perspective, is no different. It doesn't mean you must giggle in the face of horrors. It just builds the basis, the framework, on which to climb back to happy when you've gone through dealing with life's situations for which you may choose other sorts of responses.

## More than Maybe

Another example of someone who could have led a happier life had she been a Perspectivist—who had all the trappings of a "good" life but was nevertheless unsatisfied with her lot—is my good friend Allison Carmen. She, too, has recently published a book of discovery of a better way to live, *The Book of Maybe,*[29] which chronicles her own escape from an anxiety-ridden life. Saddled with a genetic history of a troubled immune system, but buoyed by a loving family, professional success, and comfortable wealth nonetheless, she herself struggled with angst based on a need for control in her life.

As she writes, "My need for certainty caused me to believe that the unexpected was always negative…Yet no matter what I did I could not escape uncertainty, and the choices I made in an effort to attain certainty always led to compromise and disappointment."

It was good that she recognized her ability to choose in life, but unlike a Perspectivist, she could not see how she could choose happiness over disappointment. As her story goes, a Qigong teacher told her the Taoist tale of *Maybe*, and it changed her life. The *Maybe* tale is a quintessentially Perspectivist one, and it's worth retelling here:

> An old farmer had worked his crops with just one horse for many years. One day his horse ran away. Upon hearing the news, his neighbors came to visit. "Such bad luck," they said sympathetically. "Maybe," the farmer replied.

The next morning the horse returned, bringing with it three other wild horses.

"How wonderful," the neighbors exclaimed.

"Maybe," replied the old man.

The following day, his son tried to ride one of the untamed horses, was thrown, and broke his leg. The neighbors again came to offer their sympathy on his misfortune.

"Maybe," answered the farmer.

The day after, military officials came to the village to draft young men into the army.

Seeing that the son's leg was broken, they passed him by.

The neighbors congratulated the farmer on how well things had turned out.

"Maybe," said the farmer.

In true Perspectivist fashion, the parable makes obvious that every situation can be seen from different perspectives: some positive, some negative. The farmer here, in classic Taoist fashion of un-action, chose neither. He chose not to render any interpretation of the events, but instead rolled forward through life as it came to him. Practical Perspectivism has no issue with the Taoist tradition. But if you want to pursue a more action-oriented life filled with happiness, you can always choose the positive perspective rather than the neutral "maybe."

Ms. Carmen closes her book with the following parable, one more ancient tale of *Maybe*, but one that decidedly moves in the Perspectivist direction:

A king had a close friend who had the habit of remarking, "Maybe this is good" about every occurrence in life no matter what it was.

One day, the king and his friend were out hunting. The king's friend loaded a gun and handed it to the king, but alas the friend had loaded it improperly and when the king fired it, his thumb was blown off.

"Maybe this is good!" exclaimed the friend.

The horrified and bleeding king was furious.

"How can you say, 'maybe this is good'? This is obviously horrible!" he shouted.

The king put his friend in jail.

About a year later, the king went hunting by himself. Cannibals captured him and took him to their village. They tied his hands, stacked some wood, set up a stake and bound him to it.

As they came near to set fire to the wood, they noticed that the king was missing a thumb. Being superstitious, they never ate anyone who was less than whole. They untied the king and sent him on his way.

Full of remorse, the king rushed to the prison to release his friend.

"You were right, it was good," the king said.

The king told his friend how missing the thumb had saved his life and added, "I feel so sad that I locked you in jail. That was such a bad thing to do."

"No! Maybe it's good!" responded his delighted friend.

"Oh, how could it be good, my friend? I did a terrible thing to you while I owe you my life."

"Well," his friend replied, "if I hadn't been in prison, maybe I would have been hunting with you and those cannibals would have eaten me."

All the while the friend, clearly a Perspectivist, was in jail, he had faith that "maybe it's good." His time in jail therefore was not spent in misery, with bitter resentment growing toward the king. As such, when the king freed him, he was likewise able to go even beyond forgiving the king, but being happy with him for choosing a course of action that perhaps saved his own life.

# CHAPTER 5

# PRACTICAL PERSPECTIVISM AND SEMANTICS

"The pen is mightier than the sword."[30] Suffice to say, there is power in words.

To change your perspectives, it may not be enough to simply have wants, beliefs, and desires. It is markedly helpful if you also change your vocabulary. We see the effects of vocabulary manipulation on behavior, mood, and attitude in everyday life in the art of framing, as well as the specialized field of cognitive linguistics and cognitive behavioral therapy.

In medical practice we know that most errors, and therefore patient discontent or injury, occur because of inadequate communication. Our everyday lives are not immune to this either.

Russell Bishop, a well-respected performance improvement consultant and author of *Workarounds that Work*, discusses choice and framing, which is another practical application of Perspectivism:

So, what is it that you want out of life and what's in the way? If your answer is on the material side of things (money, house, car, etc) and what's in the way is someone else (...bankers, greedy capitalists), then we have a real dilemma. Especially if you have lost your job, house, car and most everything on the material levels of life.

Surely, there are many of us in trouble, having lost everything due to circumstances ranging from hurricanes and oil spills to manipulated financial systems. [But]... how you frame the issue is the issue. This can also be stated as, how you frame the problem is the problem.

If you're out of work right now, and your mindset is that some dirty, greedy SOB is to blame, you may be right. The only problem with this framing is that as long as you stay focused on those dirty SOB's, you will continue to be at the mercy of SOB's who may not care all that much about your circumstances.

If your life circumstances and how you experience them are going to change for the better, how will they get better? Who is going to be at the helm, guiding the change? There's no question that improved external factors can help; however, what are you going to do regardless of what happens out there?

Sooner or later, it's going to come down to you and what you choose to do.[31]

Circumstances may be beyond your control, or events may be of your own making, but they can change and can be changed *by* you. Sometimes your external life circumstances will be obviously conducive to your state of happiness, and you will find it easy to be happy. Still other times circumstances may be equally conducive to a happy existence, yet you may find yourself struggling. Clearly, it is the internal perspective that is different, that is failing to view the moment *from a place* of happiness, not the circumstances themselves.

We often find the reverse also true. Sometimes your life circumstances are bad, or downright tragic, but you find yourself adopting a perspective of your situation that enables you to be happy, to "make the best of a bad situation." Yet more likely, at those times when life's circumstances are arguably woeful, it is understandably more challenging to find a happy perspective.

Accepting this, we must admit that the external factors of your life are not the final word on happiness. If you can be happy or unhappy in good circumstances and bad, some other factor is clearly the final word. And that "something else" is your internal perspective.

PP declares that *we* are responsible for our internal perspective, not the world around us. PP shows us that once we recognize this fact, once we accept it as true, we become empowered to choose, to decide for ourselves how we want to view the world, from what perspective we wish to look out at our life. And if you want to be happy, only you yourself can choose to make it so.

Sure, every situation we find ourselves in presents its own unique set of challenges. Your child may be ill, your spouse having an affair, your boss treating you unfairly, your home up in flames. You may be physically injured, impaired, even dying of a mortal illness. But one simple fact remains true in all these otherwise untoward circumstances. You, yourself, remain. And as long as you are still alive and coherent enough to think, you are in a position to imagine. And if you can imagine, then there exists a possibility that you can imagine a perspective from which your situation can be viewed with happiness. Recognition of the existence of this possibility is, *in itself*, a source of happiness. It is tempting, therefore, to modify the famous Cartesian notion with our new paradigm: I think, therefore I am…happy!

Still, I am not suggesting that happiness should lead to complacency. Again, happiness is not the destination. Happiness is derived from the fact that you exist, and in that existence lives the possibility that you can change, or at the very least change the way you think about, your circumstances. And no matter your circumstances, being happy can't hurt and might just help.

If your circumstances are good, being happy about it might help to prolong, or even further improve your lot. Certainly, not being happy about good circumstances represents wasted opportunities for happiness and may lead to a failure to capitalize further on your good luck. While better can sometimes be viewed as the enemy of good, it really only is true if you are not happy with "good." If you miss the opportunity to find happiness in "good" circumstances because you obsess over achieving "better" circumstances that may or may not materialize, then that axiom is certainly true. But if we pursue "better" from an existing place of happiness, then if "better" fails to materialize, we will be equipped to deal with that, too, and "better" need not be perceived as the enemy who defeated us.

So, in good times, enjoy! And in bad times, imagine good times and be happy you a) can imagine good times, and b) are alive and therefore in a position to possibly realize some version of your imagined better place.

In modern politics, framing has become both art and science. For example, the estate tax has been characterized as "the death tax" in order to rally opposition to it. This framing allows the very small number of people who benefit from the tax's repeal to persuade people who do not benefit from it to vote against their own interest. The administration of George Bush used the name "Clear Skies" to disguise a policy that actually gutted environmental protections and allowed increased corporate pollution. George Orwell warned us of this sort of doublespeak decades ago in his prescient novel *1984*.

In general, if we choose words of extremism, we will feel extreme emotions. If we choose words of moderation, we will feel moderate emotions. Words of absolutism and extremism need to be laid to rest, and words of moderation should take their place. This is much like the Middle Path of Buddhism, which advises a life of moderation between self-indulgence and self-mortification (abstinence and/or self-inflicted pain or discomfort), only semantically. By changing our words, we actually change, and perhaps more accurately reflect, the thoughts and emotions they represent.

Take the word "hate." A pretty strong word, no? Representing a fairly extreme emotion. Try virtually eliminating the word "hate" from your vocabulary. Try to find the one thing that you really truly abhor more than absolutely anything else, and save "hate" for that. For everything else, use more moderate terms such as "dislike."

If you effectively remove "hate" from your vocabulary, you will find a remarkable thing happens. After a relatively short amount of time you will find that very few things bother you overmuch. On occasion you will reflexively use the word "hate" again, and that's ok—as long as you follow it up with some phrase such as, "Well, I don't *really* hate that, but if I did hate things, that might be near the top of my list." Even better, try to articulate the specific ways that this particular thing bothers you.

This sort of language exercise may be slightly more cumbersome than the shorthand, "hate." But you will soon find you are expressing yourself more accurately, and others around you will tend to use less extreme language as well.

Hating is rather absolute, and not hating allows you much more room to find the bits and pieces of a particular situation that you actually appreciate—the silver lining if you will. For in the Perspectivist reality, there is "good" and "bad" in essentially everything, and avoiding absolutism allows you to see both sides of the coin. This, in turn, may help you find more common ground, and peace, with others who hold different viewpoints.

Words of positive extremism may be no less fraught with complications as those of negativity like "hate." It is quite common to hear people use the word "best" in their descriptions of many things, sometimes even contradictory things.

Now, as a Perspectivist or Taoist, I might be tempted to argue straight up that there is no such thing as "best." There is nothing that is not greater than something else, and there is nothing that is not smaller than something else. As such, nothing can be *the* "best." And anyway, by definition, "best" still describes only one very specific thing. The rate at which we use the word therefore becomes laughable. "Great" will usually work just fine instead.

But why is this concerning? Why is it worth mentioning? If facts contradict our assertion that something is the "best," we must modify such declarations. We are forced to retreat from our stated position, to backtrack, and qualify. We might even question ourselves, kick ourselves for being silly in using the "best" label in said instance. And this is another little hit on our integrity, our self-confidence, our strength and our happiness. We were wrong, we spoke wrongly.

It would be best—er, better—if we described those things we enjoyed or thought highly of as being, perhaps, "great" or "fantastic," literally the kind of thing we might fantasize about. Great is not absolute, it is relative. Speaking this way implies a perspective rather than declaring a definitive that begs challenging. In most cases, it really is closer to what we mean. And don't we really want to say what we mean and mean what we say?

In behavioral training, we learn to use the word "I" when describing feelings and situations in which we are involved. If one observes, one will find that many people, even yourself, use the word "you" quite often, when you really mean "I." We tend not to notice, but the behavioral effect of this curious substitution is dramatic. It leads us to take responsibility for the feelings or consequences of actions that follow. And in taking such responsibility, we tend to take rather more care in our choices. It also allows us to temper our opinions, smoothing out an otherwise over-emotionally charged life.

For example, by the time my daughter was eight years old she had proven herself to be somewhat challenged when it came to fluid mechanics. As frequently happened, she spilled water while pouring herself a glassful. When I once remarked, as politely as I could, that she might try pouring a bit more slowly so she could stop more easily when the water neared the top of the glass, she retorted, "You think I'm an idiot!" Well, nothing could be further from the truth. I believe my daughter is quite intelligent, and I've reassured her of that belief on numerous occasions. But in this situation, she was angry at herself for spilling the water, and perhaps she thought she, herself, was an idiot. But she didn't say that, and so she was able to deflect her anger from herself onto me, avoiding the responsibility of the feelings her actions led her to.

If she had instead started with, "*I* think I'm an idiot," she would likely have more quickly realized that, no, she did not think that at all. Instead, she might have then said to herself, "No, I am not an idiot, but I do need to pay more attention to how I pour." And this in turn would more quickly lead her to a mastery of fluid mechanics than deflecting her feelings and her responsibility.

Another way that semantics affects our thinking, and therefore our living and life, is with labeling and definitions. As mentioned in Chapter 4, labeling can have deleterious effects. The astute political writer, Barbara Ehrenreich, wrote an article faulting "positive thinking" in its relationship to the financial crisis that flared in 2008. As she understood it, "…the idea is to firmly believe that you will get what you want, not only because it will make you feel better to do so, but because "visualizing" something— ardently and with concentration—actually makes it happen."[32] To her credit, she also notes, "When it comes to how we think, "negative" is not the only alternative to "positive." …The alternative to both is realism—seeing the risks, having the courage to bear bad news and being prepared for famine as well as plenty. We ought to give it a try." It is somewhat unfair to define positive thinking as the belief that simply imagining a certain thing will cause it to occur. True positive thinking also incorporates the notion that *action* is required—action coupled with the belief that success is actually possible—and what success will look like and mean.

Wellesley professor Julie Norem, PhD. teaches an interesting school of thought called "defensive pessimism," which she describes in detail in a charmingly titled book called *The Positive Power of Negative Thinking*.[33] She contrasts defensive pessimists who "lower their expectations to help prepare themselves for the worst" with strategic optimists who have "high expectations, and then actively avoid thinking much about what might happen." Dr. Norem concludes that if her defensive pessimists simply try to think happy thoughts and abandon their practice of worrying themselves silly over every last possible catastrophe, they perform worse in life than if they embrace their style of thought which she concludes will help them perform better.

Practical Perspectivism doesn't suggest that defensive pessimists abandon their habit of planning for all the imaginable worst-case scenarios (though that might help). It does, however, imply they might benefit from balancing those thought processes by *considering* good case scenarios as well. They then can *choose* to move forward from a place of balance, and perhaps choose happiness because they have considered all the options, both good and bad.

Later, after increasing the amount of time they dwell in the land of happy, such individuals would likely find less and less need to indulge in the innumerable "what if's…" and skip ahead to the art of enjoying the "what's here" a little more. While some defensive pessimists allegedly achieve more success by embracing their anxiety, quite likely many others are simply overwhelmed by it. And even if they do perform measurably well, the journey itself doesn't really sound like very much fun.

Perspectivism incorporates the ideas of realism, optimism, and pessimism while recognizing that both positivism and negativism are simply alternative perspectives. Realism, while being conceptually close to Practical Perspectivism, comes up short by missing a crucial bit: how we *feel* because of, and about, what we think.

Thinking with a positive perspective doesn't make the assumption that Ms. Ehrenreich takes issue with, however: that visualization, in and of itself, makes something happen. Practical Perspectivism doesn't suggest that simply visualizing a "positive" perspective magically creates an external reality. Rather it describes that the way we think about things *affects* how we feel about things, and thereby determines how we *act* upon them in real time. Because the way we feel about a thing determines in large part what we *do*, it is perspectivization—living a perspectivist life, not visualization in a vacuum, that affects actions and which in turn affects circumstances and outcomes.

It matters what we say. It matters to those who hear us, and it matters to us, ourselves. It matters how we label and define things in our lives—because that is how we *think* about them, and how we *feel* about them. If we live Perspectively, purposefully, then we are aware of how we actually see things and we can more easily choose the appropriate words to describe our feelings and perceptions. This, in turn, further reinforces the activation of our happy brain. It matters what we say.

# PART II

# PRACTICAL PERSPECTIVISM:

# HAPPINESS, SCIENCE,
# AND PHILOSOPHY

# CHAPTER 6

# PRACTICAL PERSPECTIVISM AND HAPPINESS

Is everybody happy?! Sadly, no.

Does everyone want to be happy? Maybe not.

But very likely, *most* people wish to be happy, or at least happi*er* than they are, or happy more often. And Practical Perspectivism is a tool that can help anyone achieve greater happiness, a little or a lot, for a moment, a day, or a lifetime. For starters, Practical Perspectivism works particularly well in the moment-to-moment trials and tribulations of daily living. And used as such, it eventually becomes a way of life that not only improves one's happiness in specific instances but also advances one's overall sense of well-being.

It's not necessarily the case that one should be happy all the time, though that is also possible, but that one can be happy essentially any time of one's choosing. The perspective always exists to get you there, however easy or hard it may be to keep it in focus in any given instance.

The pursuit of happiness jumped on the modern stage in the second sentence of that famous document, the Declaration of Independence, written by Thomas Jefferson in 1776. Of course, back in the eighteenth century the pursuit of happiness specifically as an emotional state or a way of life was probably not given as much time or thought as it is today in a modern society where the fulfillment of most basic needs is generally taken for granted. As humanity has progressed socially, industrially, and technologically, greater numbers of people have been able to assure themselves access to food and shelter, perhaps even some greater measure of personal safety, and so have had growing opportunity to consider their emotional needs. Admittedly, when situational circumstances are stable and basic physiological needs are met, it is easier to spend energy pursuing what happiness in its many manifestations, but it's always possible.

Still, why happiness? Why is it important? That is, why should we not value something else above it? It remains worth questioning whether or not happiness is, in fact, a hedonistic goal at all.

What is happiness anyway, and why is it something we strive for, something we sense we are missing when we do not feel it? Merriam-Webster's dictionary defines "happiness" as "a state of well-being or contentment."[34] From our very early childhood we've been singing, "If you're happy and you know it clap your hands!" And while only the individual can say whether or not he or she is happy, happiness is commonly easy to see in others. What's more, when we do notice it in others, we wish we could be more like them. But still, is happiness a goal worth pursuing?

The romantics of the late 18<sup>th</sup> century, for example, held that a certain degree of melancholia would lead to greater development of the aesthetic senses, which was felt to be a higher good than happiness. But is melancholia really a better method for achieving this development of aesthetic senses than happiness? And even if it were, for how long should we be melancholy? Did they study it?

Of course, being generally at odds with science, they would have scoffed at such a concept, but still—where's their proof? No, the value of melancholia is lovely to wax poetic about, but of what practical use to the sentient creature is such a greater development of aesthetic senses if it doesn't produce happiness or well-being in the first place? If an ability to appreciate beauty in the environment leads to happiness, why not just skip ahead to happiness if it can be achieved more directly, quickly, and enduringly?

Alternatively, in Jefferson's day, other social and personal values like citizenship and individual responsibility were of the moment. But, Jefferson didn't write about life, liberty, and purchasing power, or lower taxes, or a balanced budget, or an early retirement. He didn't include a closer relationship with any god. He didn't make reference to health insurance or poverty or hunger. He didn't write that everyone must vote or participate in the political process, though at other times he did advocate involvement.

The pursuit of happiness, as phrased by Jefferson, is the course we should pursue when we have secured life and liberty. He didn't even necessarily specify political liberty, i.e., freedom from tyranny. He could just as easily have been referencing freedom of will, freedom of mind. For Jefferson, author of one of the most important documents in history, the requirements for considering happiness were nothing more than life and liberty. Nor did he make any reference as to what "happiness" consisted of. He left that to the individual to define for himself. It would therefore appear that, for Jefferson at least, happiness IS a greater good.

Citizenship and its consequent social responsibility are of great value in and of themselves, but more so as a means to an end: the greater good of the many. It is these conditions, established by social responsibility on the one hand, that help set the environment in which happiness is more easily attained and maintained. On the other hand, a priori, it is commonly easier and more effective for us as individuals to pursue citizenship and social responsibility if we have already taken care of our own happiness, which Practical Perspectivism advocates.

In general, the happy soul is, by nature, a cooperative soul. And the cooperative soul seeks courses of action and solutions to problems that attempt to maintain the general welfare, to seek the win-win solutions rather than the win-lose alternatives. In reality, this is what the goal of social responsibility and citizenship is in the first place—a peaceful co-existence of human travelers.

Psychological and sociological studies have shown us, in several different ways, that subjects fed hopeful, positive-oriented statements tend to be more compassionate and generous, seeking to help their fellow humans. They also tend to view the world in, and pursue, mutually beneficial scenarios. Conversely, those fed hopeless, negative-oriented statements are markedly less giving, are more selfish, and tend to view the world in us-against-them terms. If this holds true in study circumstances, where subjects have only been given statements to read, how much more significant might these findings be if we tell ourselves positive or negative, hopeful or hopeless, happy or sad thoughts over and over again as a way of life?

A new study by psychological scientist Matthias Forstmann and colleagues in Germany looked at the link between dualist beliefs and health awareness.[35] Dualists, which many people tend to be to some degree or another, view the mind as separate and independent from the body, professing beliefs in heaven, reincarnation, and supernatural spirits. Perspectivists, on the other hand, primarily view the mind as a physical function of the body. Dualists tend to see their bodies as temporary vessels, and their minds—their spirits—as something that continues on regardless of what happens to their bodies. As such, they would be expected to be less careful with their bodies— more neglectful of their fitness and health.

Forstmann used lab techniques to activate dualism in some subjects and to diminish dualist thought in others, while tracking various health indicators. Dualists were *less* healthy on every measure. They trended to reckless attitudes toward health and exercise and ate demonstrably less healthy foods by choice. They even described themselves as less focused on their own health. Subjects encouraged to mitigate dualist thought scored oppositely on all these measures. Furthermore, activating healthy thoughts was shown to reinforce these behaviors in the volunteers.

Sure, one can be happy in ill health, but it is simply easier to be happy, to experience that sense of well-being, when the body is healthy. And healthy habits, both of the body and the mind, can be taught and learned. Practical Perspectivism is a healthy habit of the mind, and therefore also good for the body of which it is a part.

In the field of childhood education, a wealth of new data suggests that keeping kids focused on character traits like optimism and self-confidence, and giving them the tools to take charge of their emotional state and their learning processes, can improve their chances of mastering the academic, vocational, and social skills taught in school. It improves their likelihood of going on to college, finishing college, and leading more "productive" lives. It increases their chances of building functional families. And while none of that guarantees happiness, such success does help provide an environment for individuals in which it is easier to find happiness within themselves.

Medicine and psychology have certainly given us suggestions as to why "happiness" ought to be a goal in its own right, from decreasing blood pressure and heart disease, to boosting our immune systems, to decreasing mental illness, to possibly contributing to longevity. In an exhaustive review of the relationship between positive mental well-being and cardiovascular health,[36] Julia Boehm and Laura Kubzansky from the Harvard School of Public Health found that increasing optimism correlated consistently with restorative health behavior, improved biological functioning, and protection against disease. Andrew Steptoe, at the International Centre for Health and Society at the University College London, showed positive affect to be associated with reduced inflammatory processes and lower cortisol levels[37] (cortisol is a hormone whose increased levels are associated with obesity, diabetes, and autoimmune conditions.). Sociologists have long told us that happiness contributes to a stronger family life, a more stable marriage, and greater productivity at work. Danner and Snowdon's Nun Study (evaluating the journals of a particular set of nuns throughout their life), found a significant correlation between positive emotions and longevity.[38]

Perhaps if we spent more time tending to our happiness first, we would be better positioned to satisfy our basic needs rather than just the other way around. It's like putting on your own oxygen in an airplane before helping others.

So we know how happiness is defined, and we know that it is good for us and to be valued. But what is the nature of this happiness that we might be pursuing, or improving for ourselves anyway? I am not talking about simple moment-to-moment pleasures of the senses—the sex, drugs, and rock 'n roll kind—though these things may indeed contribute a transient sense of well-being and are therefore worthwhile in appropriate doses.

No, I am talking about the *"cheerfulness of...mind"* sort of happiness to which the Greek philosopher Epicurus referred to over 2000 years ago. In a dying letter he wrote to his friend Idomeneus, it is clear he believed the lack of a troubled soul was paramount, and could be achieved and maintained even in the face of physical pain and certainty of death:

> I have written this letter to you on a happy day to me, which is also the last day of my life. For I have been attacked by a painful inability to urinate, and also dysentery, so violent that nothing can be added to the violence of my sufferings. But the cheerfulness of my mind, which comes from the recollection of all my philosophical contemplation, counterbalances all these afflictions.[39]

Or consider the happy life led by Manohar Aich, a former Mr. Universe body builder who had served prison time as a political dissident. He used his time constructively to pursue weight training in earnest—Practical Perspectivism clearly at work. Upon the recent celebration of his 100th birthday, still in fit health, and still working out, he related:

> I never allow any sort of tension to grip me. I had to struggle to earn money since my young days, but whatever the situation, I remained happy. [40]

Over the last couple of decades, "happy" talk has become a mainstream issue and this treatise would be incomplete if I did not touch upon some of the other prominent theories circulating. Specifically, in psychology and the social sciences, there have been several principal contributors who have increased our general understanding of happiness and how to achieve it.

I will refer primarily to the psychologists Mihalyi Csikszentmihalyi, Martin Seligman, Jonathan Haidt, and Sonja Lyubomirsky, all of whom have published significant works between 1990 and the present which have helped us understand many of the components found in a happy life. The first two doctors established an extremely important discipline within the field of psychology called Positive Psychology. Dr. Lyubomirsky is currently one of the more active researchers in that field.

In the next chapter we will look at a few of their more significant and relevant points, noting how they contribute to the notion of Perspectivism and happiness, and show how Practical Perspectivism can be seen as the next step: as a world view and a method of living if you are striving to achieve a happy life.

# CHAPTER 7

# PRACTICAL PERSPECTIVISM AND SCIENCE

Spanning the turn of this last century, formal happiness research has taken hold in psychology and medicine in many ways. One of the primary starting points for this was when Mihalyi Csikszentmihalyi introduced the notion of *flow* in his landmark book, *Flow: the Psychology of Optimal Experience,*[41] in 1990. Here he describes a state of being when one is "in the zone," completely absorbed in the moment or with the task at hand. Csikszentmihalyi found that people describe themselves as "most happy" when they are actively in this state.

Practical Perspectivism would compare flow to the meditative state Buddhist monks achieve routinely, though Dr. Csikszentmihalyi would suggest that we must be engaged in challenging tasks of great skill to achieve "flow." PP agrees that flow does feel good, that one is happy when in flow, whether aware of it at the time or not. But Practical Perspectivism goes further, asserting that flow can be achieved in *all* aspects of life: those that challenge both our strengths and weaknesses, in the routine *and* the fantastic.

My wife finds this state when she's skim-coating, applying the final smooth layer of spackle on sheet rock before the paint goes on. Flow, or a meditative state, should be how we strive to live every moment of our lives.

The notion of flow, and the glow that it yields, is truly insightful, but it really is only a description of a state of being. It is not a methodology or a philosophic construct that can serve as a guide for how to view our world, or even how to get there or to stay there as much as possible. In fact, quite inadvertently, it can end up being just another goal that people end up striving for, like love, or money, or power. Some remain chronically unsettled when they feel they are not performing "at…peak" in a "challenging task" applying one's allegedly "greatest skills." Others can get lost in the pursuit of trying to define what their greatest skill is, what they should be devoting their time to, perhaps to the exclusion of so many other things in life they may find rewarding.

Just the other day a very close friend of mine admitted to just such a problem in his mid-life, having read Dr. Csikszentmihalyi's book when he was a younger man. All these years he has been searching for "that thing" he's best at, that he should be giving himself over to completely so he could maximize flow in his life. Most everything he's done in his adult life he has evaluated through the lens of flow, and questioned whether each thing he's done was the one that would get him there. This is a very bright man, generally happy, one of the most gregarious people I know. He has close friends, a close family, a loving wife and a beautiful family. He holds a high-powered job that he managed to obtain in the midst of layoffs in his field, and he performs exceedingly well in it. But he feels he should be able to do so much more, that he should have achieved more in life—and can yet if he could just identify that "thing" that he does best.

Likewise, another dear friend whom we affectionately call PEG, short for Peak Experience Guy, leads us through the woods on an annual backcountry camping trip, can find his way into and out of anywhere, and can create just about anything anyone needs in the woods out of nature itself. His goal is always to manage the trip such that we have at least one "peak" experience, the extraordinary summit view, the gourmet dinner. But he's hardly ever sure we'll get there, or that there's not a better, more sublime experience around the next rock wall. So much of his effort is spent trying to attain this ideal that he often seems to miss much of the enjoyment of the rest of the trek.

For me, hardly the outdoorsman my friend is, I simply enjoy the entirety of the outing, from the planning through walking back out of the woods at trip's end. On the occasions when the admittedly spectacular view does present itself, yeah, sure, my grin certainly broadens, but that experience doesn't mitigate the joy from the rest of the trip at all. So once again, we see the pursuit of flow, or peak experience, while noble, can have the tendency to diminish the simple extraordinary of the rest of the day-to-day, the law of unintended consequences at play.

Practical Perspectivism points out that life *itself* is flow. All the while we are living, every moment every day, we can be using one of our greatest assets, one that we all have no matter how intellectually gifted or simple we may be. That asset is our minds, our imaginations, and we can use it to find a way to look at each situation in a way that yields the most positive set of emotions or feelings possible from the circumstances. This is how we can find flow in all corners of living. Not by striving to *achieve* flow in distinct, isolated events, but by continuously *recognizing* flow in our lives, all around us and at all times.

How unfortunate, really, to think that all those rare and gifted performers, the Peyton Mannings and Muhammad Alis, the Yitzhak Perlmans and Jerry Garcias, the Pablo Picassos and Ansell Adamses of our world may have only found happiness when they were in the midst of battle with their particular talent. More likely, many of those artists saw their world in perspectives that transmitted that sense of beauty, of wonder, of flow in so many of the moments of life around them. And yet equally likely, perhaps tragically, many of them only ever achieved flow and happiness when they were creating or performing, lacking a philosophical construct as simple as Practical Perspectivism to save them from the torment they felt when not in the grip of their particular muse.

This is the essence, and worth stating again: Practical Perspectivism allows us to see that all of life is lived in "flow" to begin with—it is not a state we need to attain through action, but to realize in all moments. Sure, there are times where it feels more effortless to recognize flow, such as when distractions are dissipated, when we actually feel "in tune" with the rhythm of the universe. But practically speaking, we *are* always in rhythm with the universe, whether we are aware of it or not. And this is true whether we are actively engaged in the deployment of our "highest strengths and talents" as Csikszentmihalyi deems necessary or, quite conversely, at our most calm, still, and quiet—not so much meeting the world head on as peacefully floating on the river, or tucked away in silent meditation.

Building upon Csikszentmihalyi's concepts, Martin Seligman published his seminal book, *Authentic Happiness*, in 2000, truly putting the happiness industry on the map. Seligman, a co-founder of Positive Psychology and the president of the American Psychology Association, helped legitimize the worthiness of the pursuit of happiness in a cover article of Time Magazine the following year. In *Authentic Happiness*, he added the notion of "meaning" to the requirements for achieving happiness, claiming it's not enough just to pleasure ourselves and reach a flow state, but declaring we must be linked to something, some institution or organization bigger than ourselves to give our actions, our lives, meaning. As Seligman writes:

I go into flow playing bridge, but after a long tournament, when I look in the mirror, I worry that I am fidgeting until I die. The pursuit of engagement and the pursuit of pleasure are often solitary, solipsistic endeavors. Human beings, ineluctably, want meaning and purpose in life. The Meaningful Life consists in belonging to and serving something that you believe is bigger than the self, and humanity creates all the positive institutions to allow this: religion, political party, being Green, the Boy Scouts, or the family.[42]

While "meaning" can certainly be a condition that makes happiness easier to maintain, Seligman seems much like my friend who is searching for his greatest strength, meanwhile missing so much joy, fretting that he's frittering away the days. Furthermore, it is simply selling humanity short to declare that only man-made institutions can magically imbue life with meaning.

It is humanity itself, and the planet upon which we live, sharing existence with all the other species, that provides sufficient enough an "institution" to which a sense of belonging can be discovered, if such a thing is desirable. And the sooner we recognize this, and spend less energy defending the differences between our selected man-made institutions, the easier it will be to accept our commonalities and derive joy there instead.

To the Perspectivist, on a simple analysis, either life has no meaning in the first place regardless of our institutional connections or lack thereof, or life has meaning in and of itself. At least, without life, there is no meaning. Remember Piet Hein's Grook warning the universe against megalomania: *"It wouldn't be missed if it didn't exist."* Either way, inherent meaning or none at all, a Perspectivist would recognize Seligman's experience playing bridge as hardly *"...fidgeting until I die."* On top of it all, Seligman himself, as a Csikszentmihalyi acolyte, should know better than to worry himself if in fact "flow" is critical to happiness in the first place.

To the Perspectivist, it doesn't really matter whether we choose to believe life has inherent meaning or none at all. We can choose to make anything we wish have meaning if we so desire, or to render any other thing less meaningful. Perspectivists recognize that all things have meaning and each is fundamentally both more and less meaningful, at a universal level, than some other.

Practical Perspectivism shows us that the time itself spent realizing flow through something like playing bridge *is* important, and times like that are perhaps critical and essential to living a happy life. Taking the time to do those things in which we find it easier to maintain happiness sustains our strength through those times it is not. It helps us be happier people for our world to interact with, and for us to spread happiness afterward.

This is neither fidgeting nor wasting time at all—it is an integral component for living a happy, and meaningful, life. We do not *need* the institutions to which he refers to serve as vehicles of meaning, though they may well serve as such. We simply need to recognize that essentially everything we do has meaning because it is part of our journey from here to there.

Certainly the Perspectivist would agree that happiness can be found in serving others. But Practical Perspectivism holds that assuring your own happiness is in fact the best service you can provide to the largest "group" or organization that exists: humanity. Arguably, assuring your own happiness may even benefit all the inhabitants of our planet, not just mankind. Given the nearly unavoidable conflicts between groups, basing the requirements for our happiness on the service to any subgroup may inevitably lead to an internal conflict which could subvert happiness, either from the denial of our service to certain groups or from the conflicts created by the raising of one group up over another.

Oddly, Dr. Seligman then seems to denigrate the pursuit of pleasure and engagement (which he previously declared to be essential to happiness) by calling them solitary and solipsistic endeavors. Nietzsche would certainly agree with the solitary part, in that everything we do is, in a certain sense, solitary as it exists to us within our own perspective. But the very notion of engagement negates the notion of solipsism. Furthermore, pleasure can certainly be shared or enjoyed simultaneously with others, or be derived from/with, and paid forward to, others—pleasure hardly needs to be relegated solely to solipsism.

Indeed the Perspectivist finds the very idea of "authentic" happiness is in itself a trifle limiting at best, and beside the point at worst. Practical Perspectivism suggests that happiness is happiness.

The question isn't "Is your happiness real, or worthy?" but rather, "Do you have a method, a philosophy, that brings you long lasting happiness? "How durable is your philosophy, and how easy is it to find your way back to happiness when you stumble?" Again, Practical Perspectivism is the tool with which we can translate these important goals into reality.

Jonathan Haidt, once a student of Dr. Seligman's and author of the 2006 work, *The Happiness Hypothesis*, suggests that happiness is not something that can be found by itself. Instead, he postulates it requires you to:

> ...get the conditions right and then wait. Some of the conditions are within you... [while others] require relationships to things beyond you: just as plants need sun, water, and good soil to thrive, people need love, work, and a connection to something larger.[43]

While Haidt's point is very well made, he more describes conditions which make it easier to achieve happiness within one's self. Epicurus would surely argue that even lacking these conditions, even under dire circumstances, one can be happy, at peace, within one's self.

This is the peace and happiness that Practical Perspectivism leads us to.

Haidt's *Happiness Hypothesis*, building on the research and writings in the field of Positive Psychology, is a critically important contribution to our understanding of the happy life. Both rightly give credence to the importance of self in the responsibility of attaining happiness. Still, both ascribe secondary roles to an individual's internal state of being—instead, they hold external conditions to be of prime importance.

Throughout his book, Haidt uses the wonderful example of us living life as a composite of an elephant and its rider. The rider, commonly the lesser of the two players, is the conscious brain; at best, and with great exercise and effort, the rider can train the elephant (i.e. the rest of our brain), to move in general directions. But it is the much stronger, more animalistic elephant, he argues, responding to its base, instinctive, reflexive urges, that is the power player we must learn to recognize, interface with, and co-exist peacefully with in order to live better lives. Practical Perspectivism instead guides us to assert, once and for all, our cognitive functions to establish reliable mastery of the beast. Human evolution has developed this tool, our brain, with cognitive faculties the extent of which are still barely grasped, but clearly with more than enough capability to definitively take the elephant's reins.

Haidt makes numerous references to advances in genetics and neuroscience, combined with research in psychology and sociology over the last 25 years that have afforded us a new and greater understanding of our brains and behavior. While it seems clear that our base instincts are powerful drivers—the strong, plodding elephant—it also seems clear from equally fine neuroplasticity research that our conscious brain—the rider—with vision and practice can modify our awareness of these reflexes and more quickly, if not equally reflexively, change our behavior. Thus, the rider is, in practice and effect, significantly more responsible for the direction of the pachyderm rather than barely guiding it or simply hanging on for dear life.

Data is critical, but interpretation of the data equally so, and this is where philosophy enters. Philosophy, practically applied, gives us the big-picture view with which to incorporate our advancing knowledge and square it with our daily life. Even when the next bit of research coming down the road blows our current knowledge away, or just upgrades it a little, a robust vision of the world, of life, should be able to take this new knowledge in stride without having to reinvent itself entirely or be left by the wayside.

Conditions in our world are persistently variable, the winds of change always blowing. It is how we *choose* to see the world from inside ourselves, not *how* the world happens to be at any moment in time, or may be at the next, that ultimately determines whether we are happy and at peace or not. Happiness isn't necessarily something we should have to wait for, as suggested by Haidt. Happiness can be the way of living itself, neither just a stop along the road of life nor life's final destination reached at our end and reflected upon as having been achieved.

In truth, much of what I've learned in life comes from Winnie-the-Pooh, whom I discovered in my teens. The poem below tells us all we need to know about external conditions:

CHOOSE HAPPINESS!

The Dormouse and the Doctor

There once was a Dormouse who lived in a bed
Of delphiniums (blue) and geraniums (red),
And all the day long he'd a wonderful view
Of geraniums (red) and delphiniums (blue).

A Doctor came hurrying round, and he said:
"Tut-tut, I am sorry to find you in bed.
Just say 'Ninety-nine' while I look at your chest....
Don't you find that chrysanthemums answer the best?"

The Dormouse looked round at the view and replied
When he'd said "Ninety-nine" that he'd tried and he'd tried,
And much the most answering things that he knew
Were geraniums (red) and delphiniums (blue).

The Doctor stood frowning and shaking his head,
And he took up his shiny silk hat as he said:
"What the patient requires is a change," and he went
To see some chrysanthemum people in Kent.

The Dormouse lay there, and he gazed at the view
Of geraniums (red) and delphiniums (blue),
And he knew there was nothing he wanted instead
Of delphiniums (blue) and geraniums (red).

The Doctor came back and, to show what he meant,
He had brought some chrysanthemum cuttings from Kent.
"Now *these*," he remarked, "give a *much* better view
Than geraniums (red) and delphiniums (blue)."

They took out their spades and they dug up the bed
Of delphiniums (blue) and geraniums (red),
And they planted chrysanthemums (yellow and white).
"And *now*," said the Doctor, "we'll soon have you right."

The Dormouse looked out, and he said with a sigh:
"I suppose all these people know better than I.
It was silly, perhaps, but I *did* like the view
Of geraniums (red) and delphiniums (blue)."

The Doctor came round and examined his chest,
And ordered him Nourishment, Tonics, and Rest.
"How very effective," he said, as he shook
The thermometer, "all these chrysanthemums look!"

The Dormouse turned over to shut out the sight
Of the endless chrysanthemums (yellow and white).
"How lovely," he thought, "to be back in a bed
Of delphiniums (blue) and geraniums (red)."

The Doctor said, "Tut! It's another attack!"
And ordered him Milk and Massage-of-the-back,
And Freedom-from-worry and Drives-in-a-car,
And murmured, "How sweet your chrysanthemums are!"

The Dormouse lay there with his paws to his eyes,
And imagined himself such a pleasant surprise:
"I'll *pretend* the chrysanthemums turn to a bed
Of delphiniums (blue) and geraniums (red)!"

The Doctor next morning was rubbing his hands,
And saying, "There's nobody quite understands
These cases as I do! The cure has begun!
How fresh the chrysanthemums look in the sun!"

The Dormouse lay happy, his eyes were so tight
He could see no chrysanthemums, yellow or white.
And all that he felt at the back of his head
Were delphiniums (blue) and geraniums (red).

*And that is the reason (Aunt Emily said)*
*If a Dormouse gets in a chrysanthemum bed,*
*You will find (so Aunt Emily says) that he lies*
*Fast asleep on his front with his paws to his eyes.*[44]

—A.A. Milne

I have been happily applying Practical Perspectivism to my life for over thirty years. Through these years I have changed the trappings of my life, the external conditions, in many ways. I've lived in several different cities, held different careers, lost loved ones, found new loves—and through it all PP has sustained me.

For example, when I completed my anesthesia residency in Manhattan I had the opportunity (I still do) to take a job outside of the city and make significantly more money than I do remaining in academic medicine. But I chose to stay where I was. Why? Because Practical Perspectivism affords me a big picture view, an honesty of self with self, that keeps me doing, wherever possible, the things that most easily provide the balanced environment in which I maintain my happiness.

Nonetheless, had I departed for a new job with new relationships and a longer commute rather than a bicycle ride through Central Park, Practical Perspectivism would also have guided me to view these new relationships as exciting challenges and different things to learn, the longer commute to afford me time to listen to books and music, and to drive, which I also love. It's not that the conditions don't matter—they *can* make it *easier* (or more difficult), but it is the baseline vision, your approach to life that is guided by an underlying philosophy, that matters much more. Without the vision, all the right conditions in the world still may not get you to lasting happiness. Conversely, as Epicurus declared, even in woeful conditions happiness is sustainable if you just look at your situation the right way.

Haidt relates to us a story from Ecclesiastes of a king who, playing to his strengths (as Seligman and Csikszentmihalyi would have us believe is necessary), "had it all" yet failed to find happiness. He goes on to note how Buddha would have faulted the king's *pursuit* of happiness, that striving in the material world is not a way to find happiness; instead, that happiness comes from within. In his interpretation of Buddha's teaching, Haidt is correct. Even in his critique of Buddha, Haidt gets it right: "recent research in psychology suggests that Buddha…may have taken things too far. Some things are worth striving for," But then he goes on to say, "happiness comes in part from outside of yourself, if you know where to look."

Here he veers a bit off course. Not so much in his interpretation of Buddha, but in his own conclusion: Practical Perspectivism show us that when it comes to the pursuit of happiness and the possible existence of things in the external world worth striving for, it is not "where to look for them," but *how* to look *at* them. Buddha, of course, was spot on. The only problem with the teachings of Buddha is in their practical application in the modern world, not in the concept behind them. Each thing we strive for, whether pursuing a completely absorbing challenge or a simple task, whether playing to our strengths or challenging our weaknesses, whether striving to give up striving (a paradox, to be sure) or striving for happiness, is a thing in and of itself that we can achieve happiness through and in, *if* we look at it right. And then, we can stop going from highs to lows waiting for the next flow state, for we are living life *in* flow.

Many others have written about happiness over the last couple of decades as well. Haidt accurately notes that "pop psychology gurus of today...[are] working with the rider [of the elephant] guiding him to a moment of cognitive insight and reframing. Yet, if you have ever achieved such dramatic insights into your own life and resolved to change your ways or your outlook, you probably found that, three months later, you were right back where you started."

"Epiphanies," he writes, "can be life-altering, but most fade in days or weeks... Lasting change can come only by retraining the elephant, and that's hard to do. When pop psychology programs are successful in helping people, which they sometimes are, they succeed not because of the initial moment of insight but because they find ways to alter people's behavior over the following months. They keep people involved with the program long enough to retrain the elephant."

Despite a growing, deeper understanding of neuroplasticity (and cognitively effected neuroplasticity at that) within the neuroscience community, *The Happiness Hypothesis* concludes that there are but three existing ways we can change the elephant part of our brains: meditation, medication, and Cognitive Behavioral Therapy (CBT). The good news is, all of these work to some degree, and for some people. The unfortunate news is, none of these actually represent a paradigm shift in your philosophical outlook on the world that you can easily bring to bear moment to moment throughout your day, your life.

Meditation is wonderful in that it gives you a place to go to transiently achieve a perspective change. And it does seem to be true, as we'll see shortly, that master meditators, monks who have logged a profound number of hours, *can* actually change the way their brains function. Still, in a practical sense, living day to day in this modern world as most anything other than a Buddhist monk, is simply not very conducive to attaining this degree of meditative expertise.

Drugs chemically alter your perspective, but without the chemicals you are right back where you started. Medicine and meditation can easily and often end up as a crutch such that one finds they cannot get to their happy place without them. Many drugs come with some unwanted side effects to boot. Neither purports to represent an intrinsically different method of operation for your cognitive brain in a practical sense in the world at large (the meditative adept notwithstanding). Typically, one (meditation) is a distinct executable program you decide to run from time to time, while the other (drugs) is a patch on an inadequate operating system that will likely either stop working eventually, require another patch down the road, or perhaps inadvertently bugger another system. Neither is a new operating system.

The cognitive sciences have made great strides in this area over the last several decades, and from them several versions of behavioral and cognitive therapies have been developed and put into practice. In particular, for treating individuals with dysfunctional psychosocial behavior, organized therapeutic regimens have proven successful with specific reorientation of the individual's cognitive processing to focus more on the actual—the demonstrable present. CBT is one of those techniques that works well with people who manifest accepted clinical signs and symptoms of depression, but much of it is geared to helping individuals who are measurably dysfunctional and enabling them to function in the world. It is designed to move people who chronically persist in negative thinking to a more neutral place, to stop beating themselves up.

For example, a friend lamented that when she was growing up, if her father would tell her she looked pretty on a particular day, she would not take it as a compliment but instead, what she thought was, "I guess I look ugly most of the rest of the time." After years of therapy she can now hear such a compliment and take it as it was meant, in the moment.

It is the grounding in the here and now, as opposed to the vast and potentially wildly imagined past or future, or obvious as opposed to the potentially inferred meaning of statements or events, that seems to enable us to avoid negative and self-destructive emotions. This in turn leads to a more productive and hopefully happier existence.

That it works to any degree is testament to the growing understanding that at least some part of the human brain can be retrained. CBT seems to be working on the elephant, the emotional side of things, in the hopes that behavioral and cognitive changes will follow. But ultimately, CBT is designed to change the way one thinks about one's thoughts. PP, on the other hand, teaches us to think different thoughts in the first place. Practical Perspectivism teaches us to change the rider—and if we can make that change, the elephant, while still significant and strong, will follow.

Drawing from these concepts, Practical Perspectivism expands upon them and opens them up to everyone. There's no need for a clinical diagnosis of psychosocial abnormalities. Everyone can use a little help now and then, right? We do not ignore the value and the need to maintain a healthy focus on the actual, but we also encourage a great respect for the imaginative power of the human mind. It is simply a matter of directing our imagination in constructive, productive, emotionally uplifting—or at least neutrally stabilizing—directions, by choice and directed effort rather than thoughtlessly allowing our imagination to become enamored and consumed by the perhaps equally valid "dark side."

Practical Perspectivism ultimately may be able to be developed into a therapeutic program for the same set of psychological diagnoses as CBT, as well as to the general public as offered here. But that's for another discussion. I remain open to that possibility. For now, though, it would seem to suffice as an operating system to soften the edges of an otherwise fast-paced, highly stressful world.

To reference a bit more of the ongoing work in the psychology research spectrum, Sonja Lyubomirsky, Professor at the University of California, Riverside, deserves attention. Dr. Lyubomirsky first published *The How of Happiness* in 2008 and has numerous other publications on the subject as well. She maintains a Positive Psychology Laboratory at the university and is involved in a host of ongoing investigations.

From her website we find that her lab is pursuing concepts near and dear to Practical Perspectivism. These include both the "how to" of happiness, with topics such as: "*Mechanisms of Sustainable Change in Long-Term Positive Affect*;" and "*Mediators and Moderators of the Effects of Activity-Based Happiness-Increasing Interventions*;" as well as the social/moral reasons why happiness is worth pursuing, such as "*Individual and Societal Benefits of Happiness and Positive Affect.*"

In *The How of Happiness*, Lyubomirsky reminds us again that living happy is an active, engaged existence as opposed to one of just sitting back and waiting for the conditions to arrive:

> But what precisely can we do to hasten or bolster such increases in happiness? The answer lies in the pie chart theory of happiness...If we observe genuinely happy people, we shall find that they do not just sit around being contented. They make things happen. They pursue new understandings, seek new achievements, *and control their thoughts and feelings (emphasis added)*. In sum, our intentional, effortful activities have a powerful effect on how happy we are, over and above the effects of our set points and the circumstances in

which we find themselves. If an unhappy person wants to experience interest, enthusiasm, contentment, peace, and joy, he or she can make it happen by learning the habits of a happy person.[45]

Pretty clear, and hard to argue with much, but worth a little dissection nonetheless. While half of that equation may seem relatively fixed—the genetic portion—recent discoveries in neuroscience suggest that even genetics may be more malleable than we thought. The smaller percent, the life circumstances, are beyond our obvious control to some degree, but our continuous life-decision-making process impacts our circumstances, so even that is not completely outside our ability to affect, or responsibility to accept.

Remember, while we may not be able to predict the tsunami, *we* still *chose* either to live by the water's edge or in the hills overlooking the sea. Those parts of our "life circumstances" didn't "just happen" to us. But lastly, and here's where Dr. Lyubomirsky comes closer to being a Perspectivist than any of the psychologists aforementioned, she recognizes that happy people "control their thoughts and feelings." Practical Perspectivism 101!

In her book, she further describes 12 activities of happy people, reminiscent of several of the ideas in Seligman's works. Two of the first include:

Counting your blessings: Expressing gratitude for what you have; and,
Cultivating optimism: …imagine…the best possible future for yourself, or **practicing to look at the bright side of every situation** (emphasis added).

It may not be blatantly obvious on the surface, but even the first of these activities requires practicing Practical Perspectivism. In order to count something as a blessing, one needs to look at that thing from a perspective in which it appears to be such. Many wealthy people have cited their riches as a curse, for example, rather than a blessing, per se.

As for the second item, Lyubomirsky writes like a Perspectivist. She also pays homage to the growing knowledge base that practicing these activities, like repetition with any sport or instrument, can improve our ability to achieve the desired state of performance. If it were so that the circumstances, the environment, the "conditions" must be right before happiness comes, it would seem to follow, contrary to the thesis of PP, we might not always be free to *choose* happiness whenever we like, conditions be damned.

It is worth noting that free will itself has come under attack from psychologists, philosophers, and neuroscientists over the last few decades. Many of these thinkers cite experiments like those performed by Benjamin Libet in the 1970s-80s.[46] Those experiments suggested areas of the brain initiating "action events" light up on scans by as much as a few hundred milliseconds prior to cortical regions (the thinking, awareness parts) of the brain notice those action-oriented parts taking action. But to believe this type of data negates the existence of free will is, on many levels, an incomplete understanding of this otherwise interesting phenomenon.

First, at its most basic level, it is naïve to think we understand *all* there is to know about the brain function. We may yet find cortical neuronal activity that initiates the action center which we currently find preceding and feeding information on to the cortical areas of consciousness. Second, some postulate, as Libet himself came to do over his further years of research, a sort of mental field where the simultaneity of thoughts and actions exist in an ever evolving interplay rendering the point as to which really "comes first" indeterminable.

For those who would have done away with free will, they nonetheless readily admit to, at least, the notion of a complex brain receiving and processing information and spitting out responses. Current neuroscientific research continues to shed light on the workings of that brain. It has been shown that the advanced frontal lobe of the human brain, one of the primary evolutionary developments that distinguish us among sentient creatures, is integral in processing, integrating, modulating, and directing our choices and actions. This frontal lobe also feeds back to our emotional centers affecting how we feel.

What may appear in Libet's early studies to be a delayed notification of the cortex of a consciousness-bypassed "predetermined" action by a reactionary brain may, instead, be a well-considered, chosen, sequence of intracranial events initiated and modulated by a high functioning free will practitioner! That the "awareness" center of the brain responsible for monitoring function is notified, or perhaps updated if you will, thereafter is hardly surprising: we cannot very well know that we've moved our arm to swat away a fly, say, *before* we've actually moved it.

It's become clear that much of the subconscious "reacting" we seem to do can be brought under ever greater conscious management if we practice doing so. Journalist Sharon Begley writes about Dr. Richard Davidson's fantastic research with Tibetan monks and their meditative practices and mindfulness.[47] Davidson's research suggests that being happy is something we can learn, much like playing a musical instrument or a sport—all it really requires is a commitment to practicing. Of course, an underlying belief we have the capacity to accomplish these things to some degree of proficiency at least does help tremendously.

Furthermore, Davidson notes that some of our more "instinctive" evolutionarily developed fright-or-flight responses, which engage us to run from the tiger that jumped out from behind the tree, no longer have the same biologic/genetic, evolution-based, benefit they had millennia ago. Accordingly, learning to speed our recovery from these otherwise stress-provoking, happiness-derailing responses—or better still, learning to be present, mindful and aware, to *stave off* these counterproductive and potentially physiologically harmful responses—is psychologically and physiologically beneficial. We are doing ourselves a huge favor.

The practice of being mentally present consists of paying attention to the world around us. It requires tuning in, as it were, in both the most expansive and specific ways possible. A clear example of this heightened attention and awareness can be seen at many live music performances, particularly improvisational ones like jazz and jam band rock n' roll concerts.

Often, musicians have an idea of where they want to get to in the course of their improvisation and they choose, at every moment of their playing, how to pace their tempo, what note or beat to play next, in order to get there in an aesthetically desirable way. At the same time they are taking in the output of music from their fellow musicians, as well as the emotion and the energy level of the audience which is simultaneously providing feedback that gets incorporated into the flow of music, and updating their choice of note and rhythm. Commonly they are performing these choices at fantastic speeds, much like "flow", so much so they themselves might be tempted to offhandedly say they were well beyond "thinking" about what they are doing in any classic sense.

But certainly it is not some rogue part of the brain that is merely responding in a predetermined manner. Instead, it is a highly competent physical act performed precisely and intentionally for specific effect. It is the free will of several individuals who chose to be in a band together with specific musicians and not others, who chose to be performing at a given moment and at a given location based on a myriad of factors that were carefully and purposefully considered and decided upon, who chose the song or jam to perform at that juncture of the event, and who might yet choose to veer off on another tangent based on the ongoing input of all stimuli around them. This is hardly the stuff of determinism, whether or not the cortex knows the order of firing of every synapse and quantity and balance of every neurotransmitter involved on a physiologic level.

One could theorize that if the strength and vector of every bit of energy in the universe could be measured at a given moment, one could predict all future events moving forward in time from that moment. If we could determine every force acting upon us at any moment, and every force acting upon those forces on to our past ad infinitum, perhaps we might prove some version of determinism (that is, the location of a quanta of energy a few hundred nanoseconds down the road, for example, as if it were "fated" to be there) and the absence of free will. But we cannot perform such measurements. So even if it were theoretically possible to do so, all we would be left with for the time being at the very least, would be a relative free will, that is, the freedom to act as if, and believe, we had such freedom.

However, modern science doesn't even suspect that all aspects of the energy of the universe *are* measurable. Nor can we account for the profoundly complex interplay of neurons and neurotransmitters in an individual human brain and how such interactions leave open a multiplicity of possible actions, behaviors, and responses on the part of each individual. Finally, add to this the interplay of our experiences and how they further feedback to, and affect, our future brain function.

Thus, since we can neither measure all forces, nor yet do we understand the range of interplay of our millions of neurons (let alone all the electrons and subatomic particles comprising those neurons), for all intents and purposes at the level of our conscious mind we are *obliged* to carry on as if free will is in play. To do otherwise would be to remove all responsibility from each individual, all autonomy of self.

This is so because there can be no partial determinism where some things are declared to be fated and some are not. Determinism is an all–or-nothing condition. The laws of nature, of energy, cannot be cavalierly ignored just because we may not want to own up to the responsibility free will demands. No, either everything in the universe has been determined, forever and in all things, or nothing has, because to allow for the random to interact with the allegedly determined would serve to render the determined indeterminable—they simply cannot exist simultaneously.

Sure, we can make educated guesses, predictions, based on the above-mentioned laws of nature, about events that will happen next: if I toss a ball gently straight up into the air, I can be pretty certain it will come straight back down to my waiting hand and I will catch it. The ball could be *perceived* to be fated to land in my hand. We can enhance the conditions, increase the likelihood of our predicted outcome: tell me you will give me a thousand dollars if the ball lands in my hand and I'll have further motivation. But if an earthquake, unpredictable as they are as to the precise second of occurrence and exact epicenter location, were to occur right under my feet while that ball was in flight, I would be thrown to the ground with the shock wave and my hand would not be there waiting for the ball to come down.

The ball, instead, might bounce away harmlessly, however much one might have, previously, predicted that ball to be "fated" to land in my hand. It would simply be another example of the awesomely complex energy of the universe momentarily gaining the upper hand over me in my personal pursuit of gaining mastery. That I accepted the wager was my *choice*, knowing full well acts of nature occur. "Fate" has no place being invoked every time we fail to account for the circumstances.

Or suppose I was playing pool—a game of very specific geometric and physical principles where force, vector, and angle are all calculable. I am lining up my shot to win the game. A pretty woman walks past the table. I notice. Do I lose my concentration? Do I remember to re-focus on the shot? Am I distracted and miss? Or is my focus enhanced because I am moved to impress?

Certain neurochemical changes are happening in my brain, different than they would have if the woman had not passed, had not decided of *her* own free will moments earlier to go to the bar now instead of later, but before my brain triggers the purposeful action of striking the ball. Or these changes may be taking place even *after* my mid-prefrontal cortex fires (allegedly initiating the action to strike the cue ball) but before my hands complete the task. My consciousness-containing cortex gets one last opportunity to press the pause button—the "free won't" of the free will spectrum—to re-focus. If I am in the moment, a believer in free will, I can exercise that pause function, calm chemicals in my brain, take a deep breath, make the shot, and win the game. Carpe diem!

This notion carries with it both unlimited freedom and absolute accountability. Every action has a reaction. Every choice has a consequence. And while we may not be ultimately responsible for another's chosen perspective, we are accountable for the course we have charted that has impacted their environment, which in turn has had a hand in developing their perspective, and in the end comes back to affect your own environment.

Ms. Begley further wrote about Dr. Davidson's monk studies, referencing a particularly experienced meditation adept, Matthieu Ricard:

> I think the reason why we emphasize mental training is the realization that outer conditions are important contributive factors to our well-being or suffering. But in the end, the mind can override that. You can retain inner strength and well-being in very difficult situations, and you can be totally a wreck where apparently everything seems perfect. Knowing that, what are the inner conditions for well-being and for suffering? That's what mental training

is about, trying to find antidotes to suffering and to afflictive mental states—antidotes that let you deal with the arising of hatred, for example, to dissolve it before it triggers a chain reaction. Mental training is gradually going to change the baseline. It is the most fascinating endeavor we can conceive. Mind training is the process of becoming a better human being for your own sake and for the sake of others.

This is supremely important because in the very next step of life, the perspectives that others hold and with which *they* view events surrounding us ourselves, further determine the environments in which *we* go on to exist, thus boomeranging back to affect our own perspective. It's a relatively simple feedback loop. The interconnectedness of our universe is another way of expressing the circle of life. Nothing, and no one, exists in a vacuum. (Or more appropriately, we do exist in a vacuum; it's just that the entirety of the universe exists simultaneously in the same vacuum.) Accordingly, while we may not be ultimately *responsible* for the behaviors and feelings of another, we *can* and routinely *do,* have an impact on them. Therefore we are encouraged, out of sheer self-interest if nothing else, to have the best possible effect on others that we can manage.

Begley has Dr. Davidson summing up his own understanding of his neuroplasticity research, and here he sounds like he's been studying the Ten Precepts of Practical Perspectivism:

The message I take from my own work is that I have a choice in how I react, that who I am depends on the choices I make, and that who I am is therefore my responsibility.

Being "good" brings its own reward, and so does being bad! It may not always seem so in an $A + B = C$ kind of way, and it may not seem to work obviously every time, but rest assured that is *exactly* what's going on. Karma is sometimes instant, but sometimes not. Nonetheless, whether we can see the connections clearly or not, the principle holds invariably true. It's about an environment you exist in and simultaneously act upon. When a stone is dropped into a pool of water, you may not be affected by the first ring of ripples or the second. But the ripple down the road that brings the prize to your hand has been initiated, even if you didn't see the stone fall itself. The only question is, is your hand (mind) open to grasp it or not? That is your choice.

Having mentioned karma, which is essentially a Buddhist concept, let's talk briefly here about another Buddhist concept known as mindfulness. This aspect of Buddhist practice has taken some root in western life even without the other trappings of the religion. Mindfulness, or awareness, is the practice of attentiveness to the present moment and to the actuality of life. Meditation is commonly used to achieve mindfulness. But as Buddha conceived it as part of the eightfold path, mindfulness should be established, practiced, and maintained as much as possible, moment-to-moment, throughout every day of life. These are the same goals the Perspectivist strives for as well.

Keep your thoughts positive,
because your thoughts become your words.
Keep your words positive,
because your words become your behavior.
Keep your behavior positive,
because your behavior becomes your habits.
Keep your habits positive,
because your habits become your values.
Keep your values positive,
because your values become your destiny.[48]

—Mahatma Gandhi

A whole field of Mindfulness-Based Stress Reduction (MBSR) has been developed and is presently being studied by scientists. Mindfulness has been shown to be effective in reducing the impact of some psychiatric disorders and alleviating pain and suffering in patients with cancer and other chronic illnesses.

MRI studies by Holzel, et al, show increases in gray matter (the brain stuff that does all the thinking and action initiation) in the areas that manage emotion and cognition in subjects practicing mindfulness exercises compared to those who do not.[49] Scans were performed on sixteen healthy, previously meditation-naïve individuals before and after they underwent the eight-week program. Specifically, analyses confirmed significant increases in gray matter concentration in brain regions involved in learning and memory processes, emotion regulation, self-referential processing, and perspective-taking in the MBSR group compared with the group who did not undergo the program.

Jon Kabat-Zinn, Ph.D., the founder of the Center for Mindfulness in Medicine, Health Care, and Society at the University of Massachusetts Medical School and its associated Stress Reduction Clinic instructs us:

> ...to interface with this moment in full awareness, with the intention to embody as best we can an orientation of calmness, mindfulness, and equanimity right here and right now.[50]

Practical Perspectivism believes deeply in mindfulness, exhorting its practitioners to move from the notion of the occasional "fix" of intermittent meditation to living life, effectively, in a continual meditative state. The Perspectivist may transit occasionally away from the momentary actuality of their immediate existence to envision a state of emotion or a perspective not initially recognized in order to find their way back to, or navigate onward in, happiness. But this is understood to be part of the mindfulness process itself rather than a deviation from it.

Like the Perspectivist, the Stress Reduction Clinic website reminds us:

> Fortunately, mindfulness is not something that you have to "get" or acquire. It is already within you—a deep internal resource available and patiently waiting to be released...[51]

For those of us who do truck with the notion that, for all intents and purposes of living daily life, free will is alive and well, we will admit it does appear that many do seem to effectively, sadly, abdicate their freedom in this regard. This is an oversimplification of course: the reality is, allowing oneself to be buffeted by the currents of events is still an exercise of free will, a choosing to minimize conscious choice.

So we see that our life's circumstances are not the overriding determining factor for happiness, nor is it necessarily the activities we're involved in or our strengths and talents, though as has been discussed, all these factors can help *set up* an environment in which it is easier to attain, maintain, and regain happiness. Since happiness and well-being are *internal* emotional and psychological states, external states cannot possibly be the final determinant, only contributory at best. As described by Positive Psychology proponents and many others, having friends, meaningful relationships, etc. all contribute to an environment in which happiness is more easily obtained, but the idea of achieving this environment and then waiting around for happiness to happen is far too passive and constraining for the Practical Perspectivist.

PP empowers us to gain, or regain, essentially at will, an internal balanced or happy state under essentially any external circumstances. Of course, as previously described, some situations almost demand alternative responses, but shortening the time back to a happy place is what PP allows us to do. Mind you, PP actually allows you to choose whatever state of mind, of existence, you wish. It's just that invariably, usually sooner than later, we find ourselves wanting to be happy, or at least happier, especially when we are not. And Practical Perspectivism provides that framework.

One can purport that science, in particular neuroscience, and psychology strive to deconstruct the mechanical process of *how* our brains function in an interactive way with our environment and to construct reliable programs and processes for individuals, or groups, to focus on functional (as opposed to dysfunctional) behaviors. Alternatively, philosophy is both the pursuit, and description, of *what* we think, how we try to decipher grand questions, perhaps unknowable, such as the nature of existence or the meaning of life. Practical Perspectivism, then, is a sort of bridge between science and philosophy. It has as its roots humanity's philosophical deliberations and builds its applications to our daily lives from psychological principles.

# CHAPTER 8

# PRACTICAL PERSPECTIVISM AND PHILOSOPHY

Perspectivism is already an established, if not mainstream, school of philosophical thought generally associated with Friedrich Nietzsche, but also expounded upon by other noted thinkers including Leibniz, Husserl, Heidegger, and Merlau-Ponty. Nietzsche, most notably wrote about Perspectivism in the late nineteenth century.[52] Nietzsche held forth that "truth" can only be determined from a given perspective; that is, there is not one overarching viewpoint that yields an "absolute truth" about a given thing. He describes these perspectives as having their basis in many places including our culture, our gender, and our senses.

Accordingly, Nietzschean Perspectivism calls into question the very notion of a simple objective declaration. An individual's observations, or even an entire culture's position on an issue can never escape the subjective background which led the observer, or culture, to their conclusions. By extension, there can be no knowing objective facts, or knowing of anything in and of itself, since all knowing of any such thing is done by the observer outside of the thing itself.

Again, this negates the possibility of absolute truths and calls for continual re-evaluation of our worldview as new perspectives, even those of other individuals, become apparent. "Truth" in this way is an evolving paradigm by its very nature, rather than a static, knowable endpoint.

We are always adopting perspectives whether we are aware of it or not. That an individual's perception of existence is affected by the circumstances surrounding them doesn't absolve them of the final choice of their applied perspective of those circumstances. Truth is made by, not for, individuals and peoples. In the posthumously assembled collection *The Will to Power*, Nietzsche notes:

> In so far as the word "knowledge" has any meaning, the world is knowable, but it is interpretable otherwise; it has no meaning behind it, but countless meanings.[53]

This leads to the underlying belief that, while arguing philosophically against an absolute truth in his Perspectivism, Nietzsche understood that life had to be lived by real beings:

> Although Nietzsche has made it clear that we can never know an absolute…Just because one does not know that one's beliefs are true does not mean that one should not forcefully will them to be true. Indeed, if there is no transcendental truth, we are given the freedom to create truth as we want it to be.[54]

Similarly, in *On the Genealogy of Morality: A Polemic,* Nietzsche actually utilizes the notion of perspectives, attesting to their multiplicity and the benefit of looking for them:

> There is only perspectival seeing, only perspectival "knowing"; and the more affects we allow to speak about a matter, the more eyes, different eyes, we know how to bring to bear on one and the same matter, that much more complete will our "concept" of this matter, our "objectivity" be.[55]

This is to say, as the Practical Perspectivist would agree, that the more we recognize our own momentary viewpoint as a unique individual perspective and only part of the essentially infinite nature of a thing, the more we are in a position to open our minds to the plethora of perspectives engendered by said thing, thus increasing our overall understanding of it, and by extension, of our world.

Perspective itself is defined as "a mental view or prospect."[56] It is our way of looking at our world, past, present, and future. We take our current circumstances, overlay our past experience and accumulated knowledge, sprinkle on our hopes and fears, and come up with a mental view or prospect, a perspective, on our situation. From there, we decide how to move forward, how to act. This sort of calculation commonly takes place nearly reflexively, but can also be thoroughly considered with purposeful awareness—and often is.

The notion underlying Nietzschean Perspectivism, that knowledge and truth exist only in the eye of the beholder, is completely respected in Practical Perspectivism. However, whereas Nietzsche's musings are a tool with which to argue philosophically about the nature of truth, Practical Perspectivism is a tool with which to live everyday life. On a daily basis we have little need to be worried about subtle paradoxes in abstract discussions about absolute truth. What we desire is an ethical and emotional compass that helps us find, and stay on, a path of peace and happiness. We seek a way of life that helps us maintain our equilibrium through otherwise trying times and allows us to enjoy fully, to be present completely, in the remaining times of relative ease.

Now that a main underlying concept of Practical Perspectivism, the Nietzschean idealized version, has been fleshed out, it is important to return briefly to the Cult of the Individual. This was referenced during the discussion of Precept 6: *You are always free to choose a new perspective and, with that, new feelings.* It is important to distinguish that Practical Perspectivism does not advocate on behalf of the Cult of the Individual. Characterized as a mind-set that the individual has interests at odds with others and society in general—one in which the individual is entitled to legislate unto itself what is best for itself in order to legitimize the pursuit of interests that may be of harm to themselves or society—the modern Cult of the Individual is naught but an ill-considered application of some of the ideas embodied in PP.

In no way does Practical Perspectivism suggest unfettered selfishness is a productive course to follow. While it is true we cannot but act in our own interest, living without regard to others ends up not being to our maximum benefit. As it turns out, in most common circumstances, interests and pursuits followed that do *not* run counter to society's interests in general—at least in a relatively free society—are most capable of setting up environments in which our own individual happiness is most attainable and sustainable.

That said, as it happens, the father of the Cult of the Individual, Emile Durkheim, who wrote of it in his *The Division of Labour in Society* in the late 1800s, actually railed against the modern day egoistic version of the Cult:

> The task of the most advanced societies is, then, a work of justice... to make social relations always more equitable, so as to assure the free development of all our socially useful forces... and for that it is necessary for the external conditions of competition to be equal. If, moreover, we remember that collective conscience is becoming more and more a cult of the individual, we shall see that what characterizes the morality of organized societies...that there is something more human, therefore, more rational, about them...it only asks that we be thoughtful of our

fellows and that we be just, that we fulfill our duty, that we work at the function we can best execute and receive the just reward for our services.[57]

It is clear that, as conceived by Durkheim, serving one's self is intimately intertwined with serving others.

When Practical Perspectivism suggests encouraging the choosing of happiness, it is intended for the masses of humanity, regular folk, not those suffering fundamentalist delusions, frank psychological or psychiatric disorders. Nonetheless, one might wonder if PP would encourage the psychopaths and sociopaths out there to choose happiness since their behavior is generally directed to the obvious detriment of others. Should Practical Perspectivism be let out of the closet if it might be used by the deranged to be happy about their behavior?

The truth is, though, that psychopathic and sociopathic behavior is pathologic by definition. These sufferers already display these destructive tendencies and already may feel great guilt or remorse about it (or not), but being happy (or not) will not likely make them act this way *more*. This is who they already are. It is on the one hand indistinguishable if they continue to live pathologically and they are happy about it, while on the other hand, there is no reason to deny ourselves, the masses, a methodology for the pursuit of happiness simply to keep the same from those pathologically inclined.

In that same vein, what of those who may not be pathologic, but are just plain immoral by general standards—those who feed off others without concern for anyone else's feelings? What if they utilize Practical Perspectivism to be happier about their life style? Again, on the one hand, this is how these sorts operate anyway, whether or not they are happy about it. Quite possibly, they are more happy than the general public to begin with as they seem to lack much of the social or moral conscience that commonly stands in the way of the rest of us engaging in similar behavior. Providing these social abusers with tools to help themselves become more happy still can hardly be suspected to increase their already unbridled offensive ways.

But even if it did, once again, should we all deny ourselves the opportunity for greater happiness in sacrifice? Hardly! And what is equally *possible* is, when encouraged to think about happiness for themselves, in particular to think about choice and responsibility, they might in fact recognize that others are striving for happiness too, and we might just be able to convince some of them that increasing the happiness of others can further increase their own. Because in the end, as stated before, while there are no absolute requirements (other than life, and perhaps a free mind) for attaining a happy state, it is *easier* to be happy under some conditions than others—and one of those conditions is having happy people around you. It is circular and self-reinforcing. Again, though, nothing is lost at any rate if they do not change.

That the Perspectivist may seek to promote happiness in others brings it into consistency with utilitarianism, which suggests our behaviors should be predicated on optimizing happiness for the greatest number. It is somewhat of a Vulcan (*Star Trek*) type of ideal one might hear Mr. Spock utter, where the good of the many outweighs the good of the few. Practical Perspectivism, for obvious self-serving reasons if nothing else, agrees with this notion in the general sense.

The Perspectivist simply puts the emphasis on the one thing we can control with near certainty in contributing to the happiness of the greatest number, and that is assuring the masses that we, each of us individually, will be happy unto ourselves. And since Perspectivists know that they do not have to subjugate the happiness of others in order to obtain happiness themselves, the flip side of utilitarianism—negative utilitarianism, which advocates doing the least harm—can also be satisfied without conflict.

Nonetheless, it is critical to remember, and worth restating as much as necessary, that an individual's own happiness is ultimately not dependent on another's happiness. If it were, we could all only be happy if everyone was, because sooner or later somewhere in the course of such non-existent theoretical interdependency of happiness any one individual's unhappiness would lead, ice nine-like, to everyone's unhappiness (In his seminal novel, *Cat's Cradle*,[58] Kurt Vonnegut introduced the concept of ice nine, a fictitious crystalline ice structure of $H_2O$ developed by a genius scientist that, when in contact with any other molecule of water would propagate freezing those molecules of water into ice nine as well. Obviously, once released, ice nine would freeze all water everywhere, and the end of the world as we know it would ensue.)

It would be nice if, on the other hand, one's individual happiness *would*, ice nine-like, lead ultimately to *everyone's* happiness. Sadly this too is just not the case, though it is actually closer to the truth, because happiness tends to be somewhat contagious. As per Nietzsche, each individual's own internal perspective rules sovereign and must be able to find its own happy vantage point from which to view the world. Unfortunately, happiness is not enough like ice nine.

# CHAPTER 9

# CONCLUSIONS

Happiness is…

Snoopy would remind us it is a warm puppy, and of course he'd be right. But puppies grow up, and it's hard to constantly have puppies around at all times.

Practical Perspectivism is simultaneously a philosophical construct and a simple guide to living that is grown from ancient seeds and watered with the insights of humanity throughout the ages. It is a natural culmination and fulfillment of a line of thinking that has sought to ease our human condition and to make our passing through this world more fluid—and joyful.

Much of human thought for thousands of years now has gone into trying to determine ways to find happiness, to be happy, to stay happy. A very large part of that thinking has come to remarkably similar conclusions, if admittedly along different pathways. As happy-child-rearing guru and sociologist Christine Carter says, "We think our children are born with the capacity to be cheerful or happy, and it's not that this isn't true, but happiness can also be taught like a foreign language, and just like a foreign language, it needs to be practiced."[59]

Happiness is inside of us. We just need to know where to find it, how to cultivate it, how to sustain it, and how to regain it when we lose touch with it. Happiness keeps us healthier and makes us better earthlings in general. And so, it approaches a moral obligation, if not just damn good sense, to strive toward this goal.

Happiness is something pretty much every single one of us can have more of. You might not get yourself to feeling like writing a poem as corny as the one I included near the beginning of this treatise, but you can most assuredly be happier than you are, and happier more often. And you don't have to win the lottery. You simply have to want it, believe you can achieve it, and then be willing to exercise command over your own mind. And isn't that something we all want in the first place, something that is an essential part of freedom: to be masters of our own minds?

Self-control *is* the hardest part. But every bit of work you put in to this challenge will be rewarded, and in more ways than just purely your own personal happiness. Working on your own self-control and self-awareness, being here now as often and as much as possible, will enhance your productiveness, will enhance your efficiency, will improve your friendships and much more, and all of which will positively feedback on increasing your happiness.

Buddha tells us these things, as did Lao Tsu before him. Epicurus, Nietzsche, Cognitive Behavioral Therapy, Positive Psychology, and the entirety of the self-help kingdom like *Chicken Soup for the Soul* and *Don't Sweat the Small Stuff*—human thought through the ages—all tell versions of the same idea. Certainly, some are more clear and accessible than others, some with better recipes, some more easily grasped by different peoples. But the idea that you yourself have the power to affect and effectuate your own well-being despite the vagaries of the world around you remains consistent.

I decided for myself some 35 years ago that I wanted to be happy—really and truly—and that I was going to take charge of my own happiness, that I wasn't going to let any one or any thing stand in my way. That is how Practical Perspectivism began its development, and I have been one of the happiest souls I know since then. And anyone who knows me will remark on this. As my daughter aptly says: "Most people would try and walk through life avoiding the cracks and the rough places, but I prefer to dance through life wherever the path may lead." And dance happy doing so.

Now then, if being happy makes us healthier, helps us live longer and more productive lives, makes us more pleasant to be around and thereby creates an environment in which others can more easily attain happiness, choosing happiness seems like a reasonable, and perhaps important, pursuit after all. And while the first three justifications are meaningful to us individually, the latter reasons add a moral imperative to looking after our own happiness: it may very well be the best thing you can do for others as well.

Being a model of happiness gives others hope that they, too, can be happier. Establishing yourself as a reliable base of happiness provides others with the surety that they can find, in and with you, a world in which happiness is allowed, encouraged, and accepted and one in which they may be happy as well. And a happy world is a peaceful world, a nurturing and supportive world—in short, a Humanist world of mutual respect. Taking care of your own happiness is one of the most satisfying and gratifying ways to make our world a better place.

In the end, Practical Perspectivism is a thought process that is easy to grasp and easy to practice, easy to gain proficiency with and, perhaps only slightly more challenging to master. Accept responsibility for your actions and thoughts, believe you can change them, and *do* so. PP is exceptionally empowering in its declaration that YOU choose…your thoughts, your actions—your life.

### *Choose happiness!*

☺

# ACKNOWLEDGEMENTS

This project may never have even been started but for a night at Fire Island, New York listening to the Atlantic crash upon the shore close by and my two friends, Leigh Schnitzer Wolfsthal and Lori Fields, social workers in training and practice respectively, pushing me to define my philosophy of life and happiness and put it into words. Even then the project may not have been embarked upon had my double PhD philosopher friend, the Australian and world denizen Victoria Barker, on a three-family trip to Knokke, Belgium, not agreed to act as consultant for the most technical Nietzschean parts and more. Knowing I had numerous others to call upon spanning the fields of writers, editors, book sellers, ethicists, therapists, psychologists, and legal counsel including and especially Allan Jay Zahn, Benita Zahn, Anita Simons, Billy Wolfsthal, Liz Van Doren, John Rosenthal, Mark Fields, Jane Penaz, and Chester Rothstein assured me I would have plenty of expert advice and encouragement.

Finally, and most importantly, my thanks and love go the support of my wife, Giselle Simons, the most well-read individual I've ever known, and an extraordinary artist who I knew would ultimately create the cover and internal artistry for the finished project, who believed in the effort, added insight, critique, and several rounds of editing. Of course I would be remiss if I did not also thank my daughter, Josca, for her patience with me, and I apologize to her for all the time this project has taken me away from her.

# BIBLIOGRAPHY

1. Frost, Robert. *Mountain Interval, The Road Not Taken.* New York: Holt, 1916
2. Boswell, James. *The Life of Samuel Johnson.* New York: Penguin Classics Hibbert, Christopher,1986.
3. Wilcox, Ella Wheeler. *The Worlds and I.* New York: George II Doran Company, 1918
4. Brodesser-Akner, Taffy. *The Merchant of Just Be Happy.* New York: *The New York Times*, 2013
5. Hunter, Robert; Grateful Dead. *Black Peter, Workingman's Dead.* Ice Nine Publishing: San Rafael, 1970
6. Shannon, Lisa J. *A Thousand Sisters.* Berkeley: Seal Press, 2010
7. Kaufmann, Walter. *On the Genealogy of Morals, Friedrich Nietzsche.* New York: Vintage Books, 1969
8. Martell, Yann. *Life of Pi.* Orlando: Harcourt Books, 2001
9. Merton, Thomas. *The Way of Chuang Tzu.* New York: New Directions, 1969
10. Hunter, Robert; Grateful Dead. *Scarlet Begonias, Mars Hotel.* Ice Nine Publishing: San Rafael, 1974
11. Oldfather, William Abbott. *Discourses, Epictetus.* Cambridge: Loeb Classical Library, 1925
12. Jagger, Mick; Richards, Keith. *You Can't Always Get What You Want.* New York: ABKCO Music, Inc. 1968. Used by permission, all rights reserved.
13. Arden, John B *Rewire Your Brain.* Hoboken: Wiley, 2010

14. Kierkegaard, Søren. *Purity of Heart is to Will One Thing; spiritual preparation for the office of confession.* trans. Douglas Van Steere. New York, Harper & Row, 1956

15. Dr. Seuss. *The Sneetches and Other Stories - What Was I Scared Of?* New York: Random House, 1961

16. Arden, John B. *Rewire Your Brain.* Hoboken: Wiley, 2010

17. Chopra, Deepak. *The Third Jesus: The Christ We Cannot Ignore.* New York: Three Rivers Press, 2009

18. Franklin, Benjamin. *Benjamin Franklin's The Art of Virtue: His Formula for Successful Living*

19. Lennon, John; McCartney, Paul. The Beatles. *The End: Abbey Road.* London: Apple Records, 1969

20. L'Engle, Madeleine. *A Wrinkle in Time.* New York: Farra, Straus and Giroux, 1962

21. Norem, Julie. *The Positive Power of Negative Thinking.* New York: Basic Books, 2002

22. Lehrer, Jonah. *When I Feel Stuck or Stumped I Go For A Stroll.* www.goodreads.com/author_blog_posts/2329013

23. Hien, Piet. *Megalomania, Grooks 2.* New York: Doubleday & Company, Inc., 1968

24. Hien, Piet. *Thoughts on a Subway Platform Grooks 2.* New York: Doubleday & Company, Inc., 1968

25. Hien, Piet. *Stone in Shoe, Grooks 2.* New York: Doubleday & Company, Inc., 1968

26. Hien, Piet. *Brave, Grooks 2.* New York: Doubleday & Company, Inc., 1968

27. Barlow, John Perry; Grateful Dead. *Saint of Circumstance, Go to Heaven.* Ice Nine Publishing: San Rafael, 1980

28. Rubin, Gretchen. *The Happiness Project.* New York: Harper, 2009

29. Carmen, Allison. *The Book of Maybe.* CreateSpace Independent Publishing Platform, 2013

30. Bulwer-Lytton, Edward. *Richelieu; Or the Conspiracy.* Whitefish: Kessinger Publishing, 1839

31. Bishop, Russell. *How You Frame The Problem Is The Problem. The Huffington Post,* 2010

32. Ehrenreich, Barbara. *The Power of Negative Thinking. Huffington Post,* 2008

33. Norem, Julie. *The Positive Power of Negative Thinking.* New York: Basic Books, 2002

34. *Merriam-Webster's Collegiate Dictionary, Tenth Edition.* Springfield: Merriam Webster, Inc., 1999

35. Forstmann, Matthias. *The mind is willing, but the flesh is weak: the effects of mind-body dualism on health behavior. Psychological Science.* Washington: Association for Psychological Science, 2012

36. Boehm, Julia; Kubzansky, Laura. *The Heart's Content: The Association Between Positive Psychological Well-Being and Cardiovascular Health, Psychological Bulletin* Washington: American Psychological Association, 2012

37. Steptoe, Andrew. *Positive Affect and Health-related Neuroendocrine, Cardiovascular, and Inflammatory Processes, PNAS Vol 102 no. 18, 6508-6512.* Washington: Proceedings of the National Academy of Sciences, 2005

38. Danner, Deborah; Snowdon, *David. Positive Emotions in Early Life and Longevity: Findings from the Nun Study. Journal of Personality and Social Psychology.* Washington: American Psychological Association, 2001

39. Yonge, C.D. *Diogenes Laertius: The Lives and Opinions of Eminent Philosophers.* Ulan Press, 2012

40. Deutsch, Kevin. *Ex-Mr. Universe, Manohar Aich, turns 100 Claims secret to his long life is happiness.* New York*: NY Daily News*, 2012

41. Csikszentmihalyi, Mihalyi. *Flow: The Psychology of Optimal Experience.* New York: Harper Perennial, 1990

42. Seligman, Martin. *Authentic Happiness: Using the New Positive Psychology to Realize Your Potential for Lasting Fulfillment.* New York: New York Free Press, 2002

43. Haidt, Jonathan. *The Happiness Hypothesis: Finding Modern Truth in Ancient Wisdom.* New York: Basic Books, 2006

44. Milne, A.A. *When We Were Very Young - The Doctor and the Dormouse.* York: Methuen, 1924

45. Lyubomirsky, Sonja. *The How of Happiness.* New York: Penguin Books, 2008

46. Libet, Benjamin. *Time of Conscious Intention to Act in Relation to Onset of Cerebral Activity, Brain.* Oxford: Oxford University Press, 1983.

47. Begley, Sharon. *Train Your Mind, Change Your Brain*, New York: Ballantine Books, 2008

48. Gold, Taro. *Open Your Mind, Open Your Life: A Book of Eastern Wisdom*. Riverside: Andrews McMeel Universal, 2001

49. Holzel, Britta. *Mindfulness Practice Leads To Increases In Regional Brain Gray Matter Density, Psychiatry Research: Neuroimaging*. Philadelphia: Elsevier, Inc., 2011

50. Kabat-Zinn, Jon. *Wherever You Go, There You Are: Mindfulness Meditation in Everyday Life*. New York: Hyperion, 1994

51. *Center for Mindfulness in Medicine, Health, and Society*, www.umassmed.edu/cfm/stress/index.aspx

52. Kaufmann, Walter. *On the Genealogy of Morals, Friedrich Nietzsche*. New York: Vintage Books, 1969

53. Kaufmann, Walter. *Friedrich Nietzsche; The Will to Power*. New York: Vintage Books, 1968

54. Olson, Nate. *Perspectivism and Truth in Nietzsche's Philosophy: A Critical Look at the Apparent Contradiction*. Northfield: St. Olaf College, 2012

55. Clarke, Maudemarie; Swensen, Alan. *On the Genealogy of Morality: A Polemic*. Indianapolis: Hackett Publishing, 1998

56. *Merriam-Webster's Collegiate Dictionary, Tenth Edition*. Springfield: Merriam Webster, Inc., 1999

57. Marske, Charles. *Durkheim's "Cult of the Individual" and the Moral Reconstitution of Society, Sociological Theory*. New York: American Sociological Society, 1987

BIBLIOGRAPHY

58. Vonnegut, Kurt. *Cat's Cradle*. Geneva: Holt, Rinehart and Winston, 1963

59. Sacks, Melinda. *Learning Joy*, *Scene Magazine*. Palo Alto: ISSUU, 2010